PREFACE AI
INTRODUCTION
TO THE
PHENOMENOLOGY
OF MIND

The Library of Liberal Arts
Oskar Piest, Founder

PREFACE AND INTRODUCTION TO THE PHENOMENOLOGY OF MIND

GEORG WILHELM FRIEDRICH HEGEL

Edited, with an introduction, by
LAWRENCE S. STEPELEVICH

The Library of Liberal Arts

• •

published by

Macmillan Publishing Company
New York
Collier Macmillan Publishers
London

Georg Wilhelm Friedrich Hegel: 1770–1831

Phänomenologie des Geistes was originally published in 1807

• • • • • • • • • • • • • • • •

Copyright © 1990 by Macmillan Publishing Company,
a division of Macmillan, Inc.

Printed in the United States of America

Macmillan Publishing Company
866 Third Avenue, New York, New York 10022

Collier Macmillan Canada, Inc.

Library of Congress Cataloging-in-Publication Data

Hegel, Georg Wilhelm Friedrich, 1770–1831.
  [Phänomenologie des Geistes. Vorrede. English]
  Preface and Introduction to The phenomenology of mind / Georg Wilhelm Friedrich Hegel; edited with an introduction by Lawrence S. Stepelevich.
    p. cm.—(The Library of liberal arts)
  Bibliography: p.
  ISBN 0-02-417115-8
  1. Knowledge, Theory of. 2. Spirit. 3. Consciousness. 4. Truth.
I. Stepelevich, Lawrence S., 1930–   . II. Hegel, Georg Wilhelm Friedrich, 1770–1831. Phänomenologie des Geistes. Einleitung. English. 1990. III. Title. IV. Series: Library of liberal arts (Macmillan Publishing Company)
  B2928.E5S74   1990
  193—dc19   88-27088
                CIP

Printing: 1 2 3 4 5 6 7   Year: 0 1 2 3 4 5 6

EDITOR'S PREFACE

An introductory reading text should be both brief and important. The Preface and Introduction of *The Phenomenology of Mind* meet both criteria. Their brevity is evident. As to their importance, perhaps it is enough to cite two passages, one from an early follower of Hegel, and one from a more recent scholar:

. . . it is not saying too much when I claim that anyone understands Hegel's philosophy if he completely masters the meaning of this Preface [to the *Phenomenology*].
—Rudolf Haym, *Hegel und seine Zeit* (1857)

The Preface to the *Phenomenology* is one of the greatest philosophical undertakings of all times.
—Herbert Marcuse, *Reason and Revolution* (1941)

It is generally agreed that Hegel is both influential and profound; it is also agreed that he is not easy to understand. Given the scope and depth of his thought and the complex terms of his language, there is no way in which Hegel can be made "simple." Nevertheless, it is hoped that this edition will contribute to a clearer understanding of Hegel's philosophical project.

CONTENTS

THE PHENOMENOLOGY OF MIND

Editor's Introduction

☞ CHAPTER I

HEGEL: A BIOGRAPHICAL SKETCH

In the sixteenth century, some of the Protestants who fled from persecution in Catholic Austria made their way to Württemberg, a Lutheran duchy in southern Germany. One of these refugees was the craftsman Johannes Hegel. Within a few generations, the descendants of Johannes Hegel were numbered among the Württemberg gentry, with careers as clergymen, attorneys, and public officials. Particularly known were the Hegels of Stuttgart (Württemberg's capital)—one of whom, Georg Ludwig Hegel, a successful and ducal employee, married Maria Magdalena Fromm in 1769. Their first child, Georg Wilhelm Friedrich, was born on August 27, 1770—the same year in which Wordsworth and Beethoven were born.

The young Hegel, who was sometimes spoiled by his mother "because he was such a good student," had already learned the elements of Latin before he was enrolled, at age five, in the Eberhart-Ludwidgs Gymnasium in Stuttgart. Although his studious disposition, methodological ways, and powerful memory usually put him at the head of his class, his teachers never regarded him as a boy of exceptional gifts. And, as a matter of fact, his eventual rise to philosophical greatness was the result of protracted, lonely, and often agonizing intellectual struggle.

Upon graduating from the Gymnasium in 1788 as class valedictorian, Hegel entered the noted seminary at Tübingen University, there to prepare himself for a clerical career. He did complete the required theological studies, but in so doing he found that philosophy, after all, was his real interest. Perhaps his decision not to enter the ministry was also influenced by a ministerial examining board, which found that he lacked a characteristic desirable in preachers, namely, a powerful, resonant voice.

During his five years at the seminary, Hegel shared rooms with Friedrich Schelling, himself destined to philosophical

1

fame, and with Friedrich Hölderlin, now widely regarded as the greatest German poet after Goethe. Hegel's classmates affectionately dubbed him the "Old Man" because of his studious ways, but he was certainly not adverse to a "sacrifice to Bacchus," and he was not seldom to be found in the company of young ladies. His youthful liberalism found expression when he and his roommates celebrated the French Revolution with an unauthorized planting of a "Liberty Tree."

After finishing his studies at the seminary (1793), Hegel found employment as tutor (*Hauslehrer*) with an aristocratic family in Berne, Switzerland. This was a depressing and lonely period for Hegel, who saw his friend Schelling enjoying quick success in academic circles. Hegel had a fine library at his disposal in Berne and turned his time there to good account, absorbing in his thorough way such works as Gibbon's *Decline and Fall of the Roman Empire*, Montesquieu's *Spirit of the Laws*, and Kant's *Religion within the Limits of Reason Alone*. Hegel's own somewhat sketchy productions of the period, his *Early Theological Writings*, were not discovered and published until nearly a century later. These writings, strongly influenced by Kant, are sharply critical of Christianity and express a hostility to religion in general that is not found in his later work.

In the fall of 1796, with Hölderlin's assistance, Hegel obtained a tutorial position in Frankfurt. Back home in Germany among friends, Hegel found himself reconsidering and then rejecting the skeptical and unoriginal aspects of his Berne writings. During this time, he began to find his own footing in philosophy and to lay the basis of his mature system, as we see in a brief (and unpublished) work of the period, *The Spirit of Christianity and its Fate*.

Upon his father's death in 1799, Hegel received a modest inheritance that freed him from the drudgery of tutoring. He took a position as an unsalaried lecturer (*Privatdocent*) at the University of Jena. He supplemented his income by charging a small fee for those who elected to audit his lectures (which included logic, natural law, and the history of philosophy). He obtained this position with the help of Schelling, who was by then a professor at Jena. In 1802 they joined forces to publish a new journal, the *Critical Journal of Philosophy*. Because Hegel adopted much of Schelling's distinctive terminology, he was at first thought to be simply Schelling's disciple, but this proved not to be the case. Terminology aside, Hegel was developing his own philosophy and was coming to regard Schelling as exceedingly obscure and romantic. Within a few years, the two men were in open and continual disagreement. Matters finally deteriorated to the point of their exchanging personal insults, ending their friendship for good. In 1803 Schelling went off to the University of Würtzburg. Hegel completed his doctoral dissertation and was made an assistant professor at Jena in 1805. A year later he witnessed Napoleon's victorious passage through the small university town. Like many Germans at the time, including his acquaintance Goethe, Hegel regarded Napoleon as a force for reason, progress, and freedom. He admiringly described Napoleon's march as that of the "World-Soul." From a philosophical standpoint, however, the day the "World-Soul" marched through Jena is of greater import as the day on which Hegel sent his *Phenomenology of Mind* off to the publisher.

The French occupation meant hard times for Jena and the university. Hegel lost his academic position. For a year he served as editor of a newspaper, the *Bamberger Zeitung*, but then he found a more suitable position as headmaster of the Agidien Gymnasium in Nuremberg. Although a successful and popular administrator, he kept yearning to lecture again at a university. For this, as it turned out, he had to wait another eight years, but his Nuremberg period was by no means unprofitable. In 1811 he took a step that amazingly few great philosophers have taken—he got married. His bride, Marie von Tucher, was twenty-two years his junior, yet this difference in their ages never occasioned difficulties; they were deeply and permanently devoted to one another. They had two sons: Karl, who became an eminent historian, and Immanuel, who pursued theological interests along with his professional career in government service. Hegel was always a "good family man." As his letters testify, his philosophical preoccupations did not distract him from attending to the needs of his family, and the various officials (governmental as well as academic) who imagined that Hegel might not care much about issues of salary and security soon learned otherwise.

Hegel's reputation rose markedly with the publication in 1812 of the first part of his *Science of Logic*, and rose yet higher when the second part was published in 1816. This monumental treatise, one of the most difficult to fathom of all philosophical books, is also one of the richest and most profound.

Heidelberg University recognized the author by calling him to a full professorship. It was at Heidelberg that Hegel produced his *Encyclopaedia of the Philosophical Sciences in Outline*. This is a condensed presentation (under the headings of Logic, Nature, and Mind) of the key elements of his entire system. He also prepared, from his lectures at Heidelberg, a *Basic Outline for the Philosophy of Law*, which did not appear in a final version until 1821. These two works, both designed as handbooks for students, were the last things Hegel wrote for publication.

Hegel enjoyed considerable success at Heidelberg and attracted a circle of admirers. His concern for the progress of his students and his careful attention to the small but necessary details of academic life had made him a favorite of students and administrators alike. It was not long before officials in Berlin, the new German capital, came to the conclusion that Hegel was just the person for the chair of philosophy in their university—a chair vacant since the death of Johann Gottlieb Fichte in 1814. Fichte, who developed the philosophy of Immanuel Kant into a radical idealism that accepted only the thinking self as truly real, was recognized as one of Germany's great philosophers. It was no small honor for Hegel to be offered Fichte's chair, and besides the University of Berlin was a most prestigious institution. (It had been founded in 1810 with the plan of making it the premier German university, and it was well on the way to being just that.) Hegel naturally accepted the position, but not without some careful discussion of the terms of his contract.

Hegel and his family arrived in Berlin in the fall of 1818. As it happened, his lectures at first did not strike anyone as particularly effective or interesting. But within a few semesters, as his students began to appreciate Hegel's great intelligence, his reputation grew—and along with it the size of his audiences. Students from all over Germany came to hear him, and although he could never match the rhetorical skills of such rivals as the theologian Friedrich Schleiermacher (1768–1834), his lectures were always well attended. One of his students, Heinrich G. Hotho, later an art critic and aesthetician, has left a dramatic account of Hegel at the lectern:

> Tired out, fretful, and with his head bent down, he sat there almost crouching, turning pages, and hunting back and forth, up and down, in the long notebooks, and lecturing all the while; his constant hawking and coughing impeded the flow of words, every single sentence stood out in isolation, emerging strenuously, piecemeal and jumbled; every word, every single syllable came forth with great reluctance, receiving a wondrously profound emphasis from the timbreless voice . . . Totally immersed in the subject matter, he seemed to be developing it of itself, for its own sake, and hardly at all from his own mind, for the audience. . . . He began falteringly, made an effort to continue, started all over again, paused once more, spoke, reflected; the precise word seemed to be permanently lacking, and THEN it struck safe and sure; it seemed ordinary, and yet it was inimitably proper, unusual and yet the only right one . . . Now, the audience had grasped the clear meaning of the sentence and longed to go on . . . But in the abyss of the seemingly indecipherable, that powerful intellect was delving and working in magnificently self-assured ease and calm. It was only then that his voice rose, his eyes gleamed intensely across those gathered before him and shone

in the quiet blaze of their conviction-filled brightness, while he, never at a loss for words, reached through all the depths and heights of the soul . . . I was utterly spellbound.[1]

Hegel remained in Berlin for the rest of his life. His years there were mostly spent in the manner usual to academics: preparing, delivering, and revising his lectures. He also coped with a steadily growing number of administrative duties, culminating his election as president of the university in 1830. By the late 1820s his lectures were being attended by hundreds of auditors from all over Europe. Still, this "Professor of Professors," as he was called, did manage to find time for the relaxations of card-playing, theatre-going, and travel. His students knew that they were welcome in his home, and their fondness for him was expressed when they organized a rare "Fackelzug" in his honor—a night of song featuring a torchlight parade to his home.

Hegel lectured regularly each semester, with the same subjects usually repeated in alternate semesters. In Berlin as in Heidelberg, he not only lectured on the topics of his *Encyclopaedia* and on the philosophy of law, but he went on to develop several new series of lectures—on the philosophy of religion, on the philosophy of art, on the history of philosophy, and on the philosophy of history. The notes from these lectures, assembled and published shortly after his death, constitute the majority of the twenty volumes of his *Collected Works*.

Hegel greeted the second French Revolution (1830) with far less enthusiasm than the first (1789). The first led directly to the guillotine and the frightful period of the "Terror," and was followed by the miseries of the Napoleonic wars. Like Goethe and Edmund Burke, Hegel was not long in concluding that

---

[1]In Heinrich Gustav Hotho's *Preliminary Studies for Life and Art* (1835). The passage is cited in Franz Wiedmann's *Hegel: An Illustrated Biography* (New York: Pegasus, 1968), pp. 98–99.

"revolution" and "human progress" were not always connected. Indeed, as early as 1806, in a chapter of his *Phenomenology* entitled "Absolute Freedom and Terror," Hegel had already linked unrestrained political freedom and public terror. Still, he did not drift into a pessimistic conservatism, and always expressed hope for orderly progress. He did not object to popular and representative government, and in his political studies such as the *Philosophy of Right*, he puts definite limits on the executive powers of the monarch. His ultimate optimism about the democratic process is evidenced in his final work, a brief study of the English Reform Bill. Unlike the conservatives of his day, he did not consider the bill too liberal, but rather not liberal enough—at least in regard to its provisions that treated lightly of monopolies and economic injustice.

In 1831 an epidemic of Asiatic cholera swept through Germany. Hegel retired with his family to the apparent safety of a Berlin suburb. While there he intended to complete the revision of his *Science of Logic*. But on November 14, after only one day of illness, Hegel succumbed to the dreaded disease. He was buried, as he wished, alongside Fichte in Berlin's Dorotheenstadt Cemetery.

CHAPTER II

AFTER HEGEL

Hegel is one of the towering figures in the history of Western philosophy and has influenced in one way or another virtually all modern schools of thought—philosophical, political, economic, historical, religious, and artistic. Much of Hegel's influence is actually to be seen in a variety of types of opposition to his ideas—opposition that has seldom managed to free itself entirely from Hegel's way of looking at things. This applies to such prominent schools of contemporary thought as existentialism, Marxism, pragmatism, positivism, and (in its several forms) analytic philosophy. These schools jointly constitute the majority of philosophical denominations today. Philosophers who could be described as faithful Hegelians are decidedly in the minority; and yet, thanks largely to them, there has lately been something of a revival of general interest in Hegel and a growing appreciation of the debts owed to him by thinkers of many different persuasions.

Hegel's first disciples were convinced that in him they had found a guide to absolute truth. After his death their major question was not whether his thought was correct, but simply how his thought was to be continued. If it were possible to add to it, what could be added? Two schools of Hegelians soon appeared. On the one hand were those content merely to continue reflecting upon their legacy from Hegel. On the other hand were those who sought to apply his ideas to the practical issues of the day.

The first school, known as the "Old Hegelians," was satisfied that the ages-long work of philosophy had been finished. The names of these conservative thinkers are all but forgotten today, but in the first decade following Hegel's death they were considered the "official" school. From their perspective, as devoted Hegelians usually enjoying secure academic positions, philosophy had ceased to be a *quest* for wisdom and had, thanks to Hegel, *simply become* "wisdom."

The other school, the so-called "Young" or "Left" Hegelians, resembled the "Old" ones in viewing Hegel as having produced the final philosophy; but instead of resting content with his achievement, they understood it to mean that philosophy itself was "finished." For the Young Hegelians philosophical activity—that is, theoretical activity—should be abandoned in favor of the pursuit of practical goals, especially political goals. Karl Marx, one of the Young Hegelians, put it this way: "Philosophers have *interpreted* the world in various ways; the point however is to *change* it." In short, for those of

Hegel's disciples who were not satisfied merely with teaching his theories, there was only one thing left to do: use Hegel's philosophy as a theory to improve the world. This practical application of Hegelian philosophy came to be called "praxis."

Hegel's own philosophy had prepared the way for its division into two opposing schools. From the standpoint of the Old Hegelians, it was clear that this philosophy had made good its claim of "absolute knowledge" and had presented a perfectly satisfying form of knowledge. The long quest of the philosopher, the "lover of wisdom," had ended in the total satisfaction found in Hegelianism. Henceforth, little was left to do except to immerse oneself in this knowledge. But for the Young Hegelians who confronted questions brought on by the actual course of the world, Hegelianism was a wisdom that not only could but should be directed to the improvement of the human condition. The internal debate among Hegelians as to the ultimate meaning of this "final philosophy" has yet to be resolved. But in compensation, it is pointed out that Hegel himself believed that disagreement among those who agree in principle is a sign of the vitality of the principle, the clear mark of a philosophy that stimulates continuing self-reflection. Nevertheless, from other viewpoints the debates merely suggested that Hegelianism was hardly the ultimate philosophy it claimed to be. In the eyes of its critics, Hegelianism had broken down into two incompatible philosophies: one, the Old, merely an intellectual exercise, and the Young, a rationale for social reform—a view best represented by Marxism.

In 1841 an increasingly conservative Prussian government, doubting the religious and political orthodoxy of the Hegelians (particularly the Young ones), brought an elderly Friedrich Schelling out of retirement in hopes that his "positive philosophy" would put an end to Hegelian "radicalism." But there was really no need for Schelling to be called up, even (as was not the case) had his lectures been successful. German intellectuals such as Marx and Engels were beginning to lose interest in philosophical and theological speculation. A new era was dawning in which "science" was coming to mean, not philosophical theorizing in the Hegelian manner, but methodical empirical investigation, including investigation of social and political life. By 1866 Johann E. Edmann, a historian of philosophy and a notable Old Hegelian, could ruefully describe himself as "the last of the Mohicans." Nevertheless, Hegelianism survived. In the latter half of the nineteenth century, when the memory of Hegel had grown dim even in Germany, there were both English and American philosophers who refused to consider that his philosophy was dead. In the United States, German expatriates formed the so-called St. Louis Hegelians[2] and the Ohio Hegelians[3]—the former putting out one of the first regularly published philosophical journals in the United States, *The Journal of Speculative Philosophy*. Historically speaking then, Hegelian philosophy is deeply rooted in American culture, and a major American pragmatist, Josiah Royce (1855–1916), powerfully appropriated Hegelian ideas in works such as *The Spirit of Modern Philosophy*.

Within the last thirty years throughout the philosophic world, there has been a remarkable renewal of interest in Hegel's philosophy—the "Hegel Renaissance"[4] as it is being called. It might be possible, and indeed it would be interesting, to identify a particular event or publication as having initiated this revival. A devoted Hegelian, however, would attribute it to the pressures of the *Zeitgeist*, to the spirit of the times, and view it simply as the reaction of universal reason against anti-Hegelianism. At all events, the revival is occurring.

[2]See William H. Goetzmann, ed., *The American Hegelians: An Intellectual Episode in the History of Western America* (New York: Knopf, 1973).

[3]See Lloyd D. Easton, *Hegel's First American Followers: The Ohio Hegelians* (Athens: Ohio University Press, 1966).

[4]See H. S. Harris, "The Hegel Renaissance in the Anglo-Saxon World Since 1945." *Owl of Minerva* 15, 1 (Fall, 1983), 77–106.

For evidence there are such items as Kurt Steinhauer's massive *Hegel-Bibliographie*,[5] which lists about 8,000 items for the years between 1831 and 1960, but more than 12,000 studies just between 1960 and 1975. This new interest in Hegel shows no signs of weakening.

 CHAPTER III

DIALECTICAL PHILOSOPHY

What is rational is real, and what is real is rational.

This famous statement of Hegel's is generally understood as the foundation of his philosophy. But it does not mean that Hegel was a "rationalist"—if by rationalist is meant a thinker who takes his or her own reason as the only judge of what is "real." It was not Hegel's intention to come to experience with a ready-made standard and to use this to measure the world. Rather, he viewed the world as fundamentally reasonable in itself, and his philosophy merely sought to express that ultimate reasonableness. His detailed studies of the physical and social sciences, as well as his wide knowledge of art and of the varieties of religion, indicate his willingness to let the world speak for itself. Reason did not stand above the world as its judge but was the expression of the world. Hegel greatly admired the realistic character of Aristotle's philosophy, and like Aristotle he also tried to explain and describe the world of our actual experience and to discover its inner logic. It is from this standpoint that we should understand "What is rational is real and what is real is rational."

[5]Kurt Steinhauer, *Hegel-Bibliographie* (New York: K.G. Saur, 1980).

Because Hegel viewed the world itself as the expression of reason, it is not correct to categorize his philosophy as a "transcendent metaphysics," as a theory that deals in ideal realities supposedly beyond and higher, and more important than the world of our everyday experience. In short, Hegel's philosophy is not like Plato's. His reality is the given reality, and his work begins and ends with the world as we ordinarily experience it. He denies that there is a supernatural world after which (as Plato supposed) our world is modeled and of which our world is but a flawed image. Hegel is, in short, a realist, not an idealist. It is true, of course, that Hegel is not easy to comprehend, but that does not mean that he rejected the mundane actual world in favor of some more perfect ideal world. He takes reality as the reality directly presented to us, and he does not condemn it for being inferior to a "higher" world of superior "reality." As John Dewey said:

> Viewed historically, Hegel's system may be looked on as a triumph in material content of a modern, secular, and positivistic spirit. . . . It is an invitation to the human subject to devote himself to the mastery of what is already contained in the here and now of life and the world, instead of hunting for some remote ideal and repining because it cannot be found in existence.

Nevertheless, if Hegel is not an idealist, it does not follow that he is a realist in the usual sense of that term. His standpoint is more complicated. For Hegel, much as for Aristotle, the mind and its objects are two sides of the same reality. Neither side can claim to be more "real" than the other, for insofar as each depends upon the other, neither has an "absolute" priority over the other. Hence it is not a matter of choosing sides, of being either an idealist or a realist, but rather of trying to understand the mutual relationship of mind and world—a relationship that Hegel views as "dialectical."

And so, in contrast to Plato and Kant, Hegel regarded both the mental and the physical worlds as expressions of the same basic reality. To maintain, as both idealists and realists do, that subject and object, mind and matter, or "ideal" and "real" are somehow opposed to one another is, in Hegel's eyes, the primary mistake of the unphilosophical or "undialectical" mind. Although our initial reflection upon the world does prompt us to regard reality as divided into thoughts and things, further (and more "dialectical") reflection reveals that this dichotomy has been created by thought itself. Dialectical thought leads the mind to recognize that reality is not absolutely or radically divided into two opposing realities, but that reality is also the unity of these two opposites. "Dialectic" is similar to "dialogue" in suggesting a relationship that strives toward a basic agreement. Dialectical thought is what Hegel means by "reason"—the generation and overcoming of opposition. Dialectical thought is simply thought that has been fully worked out, thought that has not only analyzed its object into particulars but has synthesized these particulars back into a systematic unity. Hegel, in his own inimitable style, has defined dialectic as "the indwelling tendency outwards by which the one-sidedness and limitation of the predicates of understanding is seen in its true light, and shown to be the negation of them. For anything to be finite is just to suppress itself and put itself aside."[6]

In this rather dense definition, the "predicates of understanding" are simply any fixed ideas. These ideas, just because they are "fixed," or defined, are unable to satisfy the mind's need for a comprehensive view, for a universal perspective that would include all particular ideas. Philosophy's need to comprehend each and every limited idea within a higher unity means that the limits (the definitions) that begin a process of thought must be surpassed. "For anything to be finite is just to

[6]*Encyclopaedia of the Philosophical Sciences*, par. 81.

suppress itself and put itself aside." The task of dialectical philosophy is the overcoming of fixed and limiting thought definitions or categories and the attainment of infinite comprehension, which Hegel called "The Absolute."

The dialectical process begins with a "thesis." This is any definable or definite reality that is first considered as an unconditioned beginning, a starting point from which all further development proceeds. But as reflection proceeds, or in the course of time, this thesis is seen to entail an opposite, or "antithesis," as part of its definition or conditioning. This opposite develops out of the thesis that is now understood as having had the seeds of the antithesis in it all along. If thought is then focused upon the reciprocal relationship between thesis and antithesis, a third and final stage, a "synthesis," comes about. This is the understanding of the unity that holds between the two apparent opposites—thesis and antithesis. The synthesis is a result of the harmonizing of opposites.

Although the terms "thesis," "antithesis," and "synthesis" are often used when discussing Hegel's dialectic, it should be noted that Hegel never did so. It was Fichte who introduced the terms into philosophical literature, and, as Hegel's own definition indicates, dialectical activity is more subtle and complex than merely ordering developing phenomena into a lock-step of "thesis/antithesis/ synthesis." An example of dialectical activity, taken from his own writing, is the best way to illustrate its complexity.

A celebrated case of dialectic is to be found in Hegel's *Phenomenology*—the dialectic of "Master and Slave" or "Lordship and Bondage," of which much has been made by Marxists and existentialists among others. This concerns the way in which individual self-awareness comes about. The process begins (as Hegel believes) when a person first becomes aware of another who is, as a person, just like himself or herself, but who is also, as an "other," very different. The first encounter of these two, who as persons are alike and yet different, provokes a crisis, a life-and-death struggle to decide which of the two is to be recognized as a "true" person, which

is to be the norm of personality, which is, so to speak, the
"master." Hegel says that the winner in such a struggle will be
the one ready to die in order to triumph over the other. The
one who chooses to live even at the cost of losing is the
"slave." This "trial by death" does not actually end in death,
however, for the master soon realizes that the slave is needed
for the master to continue to exist, and a living relationship of
master and slave is established. But the master personality, in
the course of working his or her will through the slave, will
become dependent upon the slave. The course of the dialectic
reveals that the master personality, in coming to depend on
the slave as an instrument, loses its own independence and
becomes a slave itself. The slave, on his or her part, will come
to see the master's dependence, will turn upon the master, and
in time will become the disciplined controller of affairs and
will stand as the universal norm of personality. The "master"
is henceforth the "slave," and the "slave" is now the "master." In this paradoxical manner the dialectic of thought over-
turns the common laws of logic.

At the beginning of his *Logic*, we find another example of
the transforming power of the dialectic. Here, in establishing
an ultimate ground for philosophy, Hegel develops another
dialectical paradox—one often used in evidence that his philosophy rests upon contradiction. He begins by proposing
that only the presuppositionless idea of "pure being" can
serve the philosopher as a starting point. This would certainly
seem to be the one absolutely basic idea, one presupposed by
all our other ideas of things, but not itself presupposing any
other idea. But when examined, this idea of "being," pure and
simple existence, reveals a startling complexity about it. Paradoxically, the idea of "pure being" is seen to immediately give
rise to the idea of "nothing." In other words, "being" as a
thesis leads us directly to "nothing" as an antithesis. This
unexpected conclusion comes about because the idea of
"pure being," when dialectically reflected upon, turns out to
be the idea of nothing in general. In short, to say of something
that it is simply a "being" is, in fact, to say nothing particular

about it. Nothing is learned from declaring something to be a "being." That it merely "is" means nothing. But if "pure being" says nothing of anything, then it cannot serve as a premise for any further thought. Nevertheless, for Hegel, this dialectical arrival at "nothing" from a reflection upon the meaning of "pure being" is a great conceptual advance, as it prepares the mind to grasp the fundamental unity of being and nothing. This unity is realized in the idea of "becoming." From the thesis "being," we move to its antithesis "nothing." From thesis and antithesis we come to a synthesis in the idea of "becoming." Becoming, an idea that all experience bears out, is the union of the ideas of being and nothing. Anything that is "becoming" is something that exists but is not yet complete. This particular dialectical movement, which ends in the idea of "becoming," is understood by Hegel to represent the fundamental pattern of all genuinely philosophical reflection. Dialectic is the process of thought that leads the mind from one idea into its complementary opposite, and reveals the unexpected conclusion that their fundamental truth is found only in their unity. Dialectical philosophy proceeds from the premise that true reality is a "unity of opposites."

For a final example of dialectical progress (not found in Hegel), let us consider the relationship between teachers and students. In Hegelian terms, teachers and students are two "predicates of the understanding" that, although "opposites," are what they are because of their mutual relationship. Neither can fully exist or be understood in separation from the other, to be merely what Hegel calls "one-sided abstractions." Ideally, students strive to become as their teachers (in regard to knowledge), and teachers must seek to find their reflection in their students. When a real dialogue (dialectic) occurs between them, they measure up to their respective definitions. This dialogue constitutes education; it is a unifying activity of mutual codefinition and cocreation. "Education" is to teachers and students what becoming is to being and nothing. In a Hegelian view of the educational process, teachers and students find their meaning in their mutual exchange. Students without any active relation to their teachers can hardly be called "students," and the same is true for "teachers." Teachers and students are cocreative. If they are separated, or, as Hegel would say, "abstracted" from their dialectical union, the dialogue that constitutes education will come to an end. In the final analysis, the term "dialectic" refers to a process of definition. It is a process whereby particular ideas and things acquire rational significance by being related to other ideas and things. Hegel views this process as more than a merely "logical" one, as more than the simple clarification of the meanings of words. To his way of thinking, the process of defining is also the process that determines reality—the world of particular, definite, and determinate beings. He maintains that a being can exist if and only if it is definable, that there is no such thing as a being—an unknowable "thing-in-itself"— that is essentially indefinable. As we have seen, to say that something simply "is," according to Hegel, is to say literally nothing about it, not even, as we may now add, that it exists. For anything actually to exist, it must have some specific characteristics; an indefinable generality cannot be said to exist. To be nothing at all is the same as being nothing in particular. Whatever actually exists has some specific characteristics *and not others*; it must therefore be definable in contrast to things *other* than it, as students are definable in contrast to teachers. In Hegel's terms, whatever actually exists gains its definition by being related to its "opposite." Definition is "de-finition"—a negative process of narrowing a thing down to its distinctive characteristics in opposition to the distinctive characteristics of other things. Dialectic is for Hegel a real force in the world as well as in thought; it generates oppositions and is a determining force productive of actual and specific existences. Dialectic creates the definite and definable things that constitute the world. As Hegel puts it, "Wherever there is movement, wherever there is life, wherever anything is carried into effect in the actual world, there dialectic is at work. It is also the soul of all knowledge that is truly scientific."[7]

Hegel intended his philosophy to be inclusive of all reality, of everything both actual and possible. He viewed all things in their relation to the "Absolute." This "Absolute" or "Absolute Idea" is not a "super reality," like the transcendent God of Judaism or Christianity; it is instead the sum and system of all beings as dialectically related to one another. This idea, as active and developing, is termed the "Absolute Spirit" or "Absolute Mind." It infuses every aspect of experience. In inner experience, or thought, the Absolute expresses itself in what we term *logic*; in outer or sensible experience it expresses itself as *nature*, and in the interaction of both it expresses itself as *spirit*.

The conception of a threefold division of the whole of reality was not new with Hegel; he himself believed that it was foreshadowed in the Christian doctrine of the threefold nature of God as father, son, and holy spirit. In philosophy a threefold schema had been advanced by Descartes (1596–1650), who maintained that reality consists of three different kinds of substances: the two finite substances of thought (mind) and nature (body, extension), and the infinite substance of God. A similar threefold scheme was developed under Descartes' influence by Benedict de Spinoza (1632–1677). Hegel admired Spinoza to such an extent that he was prepared to say that "to be a follower of Spinoza is the essential commencement of all philosophy"—and indeed the roots of Hegel's thought can be seen in Spinoza. In Spinoza's view, there is only one basic reality, God or Absolute Substance, whose infinite nature encompasses the two contrary attributes of thought and extension. Hegel accepts this scheme as fundamentally correct, but takes Spinoza to task for failing to see a process of interaction between the two attributes of the Absolute. Spinoza was mistaken in describing the Absolute as a static whole, as a being

---

[7]Ibid.

whose attributes stand in eternally changeless relations to one another. The truth was that the Absolute was a system characterized by dynamic change, by life, activity, and creative development—in a word, by dialectic.

Logic, nature, and spirit are the three great "moments" of Hegel's system. These are the leading players, so to speak, in the cosmic drama that constitutes the life of the Absolute. The respective roles of the three are outlined in Hegel's *Encyclopaedia of the Philosophical Sciences*. The work is appropriately divided into three sections. It begins with *Logic*, defined as "the science of the Idea in itself," which treats of the inner life of mind, of human thought. It is followed by the *Philosophy of Nature*, "the science of the Idea outside of itself, or for itself," which deals with the physical world. The *Encyclopaedia* concludes with the *Philosophy of Mind*, "the Idea in and for itself." This is concerned with the origin, nature, and purposes of human personality and social institutions. In this scheme, purely logical and natural beings are merely "one-sided" or partial expressions of spirit. The only true and complete reality is spiritual, which is the dialectical result of the interaction of subjective thought and objective world.

For Hegel, comprehending the spiritual requires the rare virtue of dialectical reasoning, which calls us to rise above the the simple and habitual requirements of "healthy common sense." Everyday thought will insist upon simplicity in the form of sharp distinctions, clear definitions, and yes-or-no answers to all questions. Such conventional "either/or" thinking is always a stumbling block upon the path of philosophical (dialectical) comprehension. Hegel viewed all previous philosophers, except the Greek philosopher Heraclitus (about 540–480 B.C.), as more or less consistent proponents of common sense. The result was that they ultimately failed to resolve the contradictions between their logic and their experience, between their ideas and their world. Until the reconciling dialectic of the Absolute Spirit was recognized, the history of philosophy seemed to be nothing more than a long and frustrating struggle. It was fought out between the idealistic schools, which maintained the priority of the logical world, the world of mind, above the physical world, and the materialistic schools, which envisioned thinking to be ultimately nothing more than a physical process. The Preface and Introduction to Hegel's *Phenomenology* are largely concerned with showing that both of these schools have failed to grasp the meaning of spirit, which encompasses both logic and nature.

Spirit finds its fullest manifestation in human self-consciousness. For Hegel, art, religion, and philosophy are the highest expressions of human life. Each expresses, in its own way, the activity of spirit in the world; each reconciles the conflicting claims of ideal and world, of soul and body, of logic and nature. In the form of art, spirit gives direct evidence of itself in the physical world. Spirit, as an ideal, is presented to us by artistic sights and sounds. In religion, spirit is presented in imaginative form, in sacred histories and symbols. Spirit is principally understood as God, who *transcends* the physical world.

The Absolute Spirit of religion is imagined as an intangible and infinite being. In art this Absolute appears in the world as beautiful. However, to Hegel it is only in philosophy that the Absolute truly comes "home to itself." In the reconciling thought of dialectical philosophy, the Absolute finds its final resting point in human self-consciousness. Human history is ultimately the story of the Absolute, the record of its own struggles to reconcile itself to itself, to synthesize logic and nature, ideals and world. It is the intention of Absolute Spirit, as the vital union of these cosmic opposites, to bring this struggle to an end—and this end is accomplished in dialectical philosophy.

The truth, as Hegel said, is "the Whole," and nothing short of that can satisfy the "love of wisdom" that has driven philosophy onward. The knowing of the truth of the whole is "absolute knowing," and *The Phenomenology of Mind* is the story of how this knowledge has finally been reached.

CHAPTER IV

THE PHENOMENOLOGY OF MIND

> In the *Phenomenology of Mind* (1807), I have set
> forth the movement of consciousness, from the first
> crude opposition between itself and the Object, up to
> absolute knowledge. This process goes through all the
> forms of the *relation of thought to its object*, and
> reaches the *Concept of Science* as its result.[8]

Such is Hegel's own description in his *Logic* of the contents of
his *Phenomenology of Mind* (*Phänomenologie des Geistes*,
sometimes translated as *Phenomenology of Spirit*). This was
his first major work, and many have considered it his best and
most important. Its subtitle is *The Science of the Experience of
Consciousness*, by which Hegel means "a comprehensive system encompassing the entire historical and psychological development of human thought."

Hegel's general thesis is that the whole of human history
should be viewed as a process directed toward freedom, by
which is meant rational self-determination, and not simple
absence of constraint. The impetus pressing this grand historical process onward is the Absolute Idea, which guides all
things to its own goal of becoming "at one with itself." Its
purpose is to reconcile its own antithetical aspects: logic (or
thought), and nature (body)—aspects created out of its own
need to become self-reflective and free. Hence, if human
history is to be properly understood, it must be seen as the
chronicle of the Absolute in search of its realization in self-
conscious freedom. Most people are unaware of this ultimate
purpose and of the roles they play in this cosmic drama. They
are the unconscious actors whose lives are played out on a

---

[8]*Science of Logic*, trans. W. H. Johnston and L. G. Struthers (London:
Allen & Unwin, 1966), I: 59.

stage being ultimately directed by an idea. Nevertheless, because they do, even if unconsciously, embody the will of the Absolute, these human actors share in its freedom and self-consciousness. For Hegel, the course of human history is not simply a long and random string of events, or, as Arnold Toynbee said, "one damned thing after another." No, history is the unfolding dialectic of the Absolute Idea. The tracing of this rational process, which is the study of the "experience of consciousness," is what Hegel means by "phenomenology." Those who do this tracing are called "phenomenologists."

Hegel views the historical development of self-consciousness and self-determination as proceeding from the "overcoming" of "crude oppositions" or "untruths." In this, he is really applying to history the old idea of Socrates that self-knowledge is achieved by a dialogue (dialectic) with others and with oneself. Socrates, by adroit questioning, revealed the questionable and limited character of beliefs that had come to be taken as unquestionable and unconditioned truths. By so doing, he hoped to encourage in people the desire, and to show them the way, to arrive at a deeper understanding of what was true. Plato, as the chief spiritual heir of Socrates, conceived this dialectical method as the means whereby the intellectually gifted could seize upon absolute and unqualified truth. The difficult path that had to be taken to this end is metaphorically described in Plato's famous Allegory of the Cave.[9] People are pictured as having been chained from birth in a deep cave. They face a wall upon which shadows of the images of real things are cast. One of the prisoners is "compelled to stand up" and turn around, and from this point on a painful process of disillusionment and of enlightenment begins. The escaped prisoner soon finds that those shadows he once took as real are, in fact, nothing but insubstantial projections of images, hardly "real" at all. When he is forced "up the rough ascent" and reaches the sunlit surface, he confronts a

[9]*Republic*, Book VII.

series of increasingly greater truths and realities. At the end of this painful and blinding path he finally sees the greatest of all realities, the sun itself. It is the ultimate source of life and light, likened by Plato to the good that is the source of all knowable things and all knowing. This knowledge of the absolute truth and reality is the reward of all those who steadfastly devote themselves to philosophical dialectic. The good is to the mind just what the vision of the sun would be to anyone daring to leave the dark comforts of a cave.

A similarly painful journey to absolute knowing is charted in Hegel's *Phenomenology of Mind*. He speaks of a "voyage of discovery" upon which "we" (Hegel always says "we") have embarked with him as our guide. As Dante in *The Divine Comedy* has Virgil to guide him from the Inferno through Purgatory and on up to Paradise, so "we" in the *Phenomenology* have Hegel as our guide. We are led through the many seas of illusory truths that tempt us to abandon our search for the Absolute. The traveler's long journey through the history of human errors is marked by disillusionment, by the sad experiences in which each of our innocent truths is revealed in its true light, and seen as inadequate, relative, incomplete, and one-sided. In our striving for absolute knowledge, we must suffer disillusionment; and during this voyage of discovery the traveler must possess a "thoroughgoing skepticism" that can fearlessly jettison all that has hitherto been accepted as true.

Because the voyage to absolute knowledge requires total skepticism, those who are unwilling to give up their own accustomed truths will hardly find it attractive. Hegel refers with some impatience to such people as philosophically unadventurous, content to stay within the secure confines of "natural consciousness" and "healthy common sense." They fear that nothing certain would remain if they were to call their unexamined truths into question. But what the Hegelian phenomenologist knows and must tell all (like the unpopular prisoner who, in Plato's allegory, finally returns to the cave) is that dialectical skepticism will lead, in the end, to knowledge. Truth is the reward of questioning, a reward won only by those who do not fear the corrosive effects of dialectic upon given and commonplace truths.

The stages of "untrue consciousness" are presented in the *Phenomenology* as successive stages of a dialectical process. The process begins with what Hegel calls "sense-certainty," with the seemingly direct evidence of the "here" and "now" of sensation. But if we reflect upon this evidence, we will come to the paradoxical conclusion that the ideas of "here" and "now" are the most *universal* of all ideas regarding nature. Simply to assert that something is "here" and "now" really adds nothing in particular to our understanding, as these terms can be applied to anything at anytime. What began as a seemingly self-evident truth, that "sense-certainty" gives us the most specific data, has been changed by the dialectic of thought into the most vague and universal of observations. In so grasping the emptiness of "sense-certainty," we have entered into the dialectical process that leads from one "shape of consciousness" to another, a process that will give us ever deeper insights into the nature of truth.

One of the later stages of the "experiences of consciousness" has already been described, namely that concerning the relation of the master and slave. Another of the later stages concerns the relation of stoicism to skepticism. At first sight, these two standpoints appear to be radically opposed to one another. Stoics profess to be "indifferent" about everything except the particular moral principles of which they are certain and to which they are passionately committed. Skeptics profess to be certain of nothing, not even of the legitimacy of skepticism, and they find no basis for confident moral commitments. Hegel, however, discovers that stoicism is the thesis of skepticism. If stoics are indeed "indifferent" about everything except their chosen moral principles, they must be "indifferent" about the question whether *other* moral principles are not sounder than theirs. And what this entails is that they can have no basis for rejecting other moral principles in favor of their own. Now, since the finding of no basis for preferring some principles over others is a key feature of skepticism, we see that stoics are really skeptics at heart and that consistent (and reflected) stoics will be driven into skepticism by the very logic—the dialectic—of their position.

In the *Phenomenology*, Hegel analyzes many cases of dialectical transformation in which a given mental attitude passes into its seeming opposite. Most of these transformations, as he shows, may be found to have actually occurred at one time or another in the history of human thought. It is still debated as to whether the *Phenomenology* is just as much a philosophy of history as a study in individual psychology. In any case, Hegel certainly tended to see parallels between the history of human thought through the ages, and the development of the individual mind.

The *Phenomenology* was originally intended to be the first of a two-part study. The second part was to comprise a Logic, a Philosophy of Nature, and a Philosophy of Mind. But Hegel later decided to separate the *Phenomenology* from the projected series, and went on to finish the material for the proposed second part into a single work: the *Encyclopaedia of the Philosophical Sciences*. This separation from the planned two-part study accounts for the *Phenomenology's* lengthy Preface; it was prepared to be the introduction to the *whole* of Hegel's philosophical system. (The much briefer Introduction was written for the *Phenomenology* alone.) The Preface thus stands as an introduction to *all* of Hegel's philosophy, and its value as such has long been acclaimed. Some have even gone so far as to say that the Preface is of greater significance than the work it prefaces. An extreme estimation no doubt, but certainly it is an extraordinary work in its own right. It has influenced generations of philosophers and literary men and women. It is also remarkable as a period piece, being steeped in the optimism of the early romantic movement, a movement whose legacy is with us still. Hegel's romantic vision finds its clearest images in the Preface, as when his own day is seen as "a birth-time," and a period of transition. The spirit of man has broken with the old order of things hitherto prevailing, and with the old ways of thinking, and is of a mind to let them all sink into the depths of the past and to set about its own transformation." The revolutionary tones of this passage harmonize fully with the emotions of the Napoleonic age in which it was written. Throughout Europe and England there were many who agreed with the poet Wordsworth that "Bliss was it in that dawn to be alive,/ But to be young was very Heaven!" Did not the rise of Napoleon herald a new age in which freedom and reason would reign universally victorious? But Hegel, still more the pessimistic philosopher than the optimistic poet, immediately introduced a cautionary note: "This new world is perfectly realized just as little as the new-born child; and it is essential to bear this in mind."

🔖 CHAPTER V

SOME NOTES ON TRANSLATING HEGEL

J. B. Baillie was the first to translate the *Phenomenology* into English. The first edition of his translation appeared in 1910; the second edition, an extensive revision of the first, appeared in 1931. The second edition has been reissued many times and has come to be regarded as the standard English translation. From it come the texts that are furnished here. Except for a few footnotes by the present editor, Baillie's translation has not here been subjected to "improvements." It is difficult to conceive of a translation that would be superior to Baillie's in rendering faithfully both the style and substance of the original German.

Although some features of Hegel's philosophy can be traced back to Immanuel Kant, his manner of writing it is very unlike the "wooden style" (Hegel's description) of his predecessor. The young Hegel, like Beethoven, shared in and helped to create what we now know as the Age of Romanticism. He wrote poetry with enough confidence to dedicate some verses to his friend, the great poet Hölderlin. He esteemed poetry as the highest form of art as well as the best preparation for philosophy itself. It is not really surprising, then, that the *Phenomenology*, for all of the strangeness of its idiom to the modern ear, has often been praised for its literary qualities. The Preface in particular is a thing of no little beauty, albeit a "difficult beauty."[10] Hegel's rich allusiveness and the striking imagery, it has been said, are not just stylistic adornments; they are essential vehicles of his philosophical meaning.[11] Be that as it may, certainly his allusions and images do set his writing apart from the arid prose for which philosophers as a class are notorious. And at his best, as in the Preface, Hegel is a writer of the greatest distinction, at once grand and subtle, who passes the severe test of rereadability. On returning to him one always finds many things unnoticed before— expressions of astonishing aptness, observations of uncanny acuity, lines almost thrown away that would be the envy of lesser writers and philosophers. And although Hegel's style, like his thought, has not always found an appreciative reader- ship, he has nevertheless left his distinctive mark upon such literary masters as T.S. Eliot, Hermann Hesse, Walter Pater, and Marcel Proust.

Hegel considered the German language, on account of its wealth of suggestive terminology, as an ideal medium for phil- osophical expression. What may be philosophically ideal, however, has proved to be something of a nightmare for trans- lators, especially when it comes to certain of Hegel's key terms. No translator has been able to find perfectly congruent English equivalents for *Geist*, *Aufhebung*, and *Begriff*, to men- tion but three of the terms in question.

[10]See John Findlay, "Hegel," in *A Critical History of Western Philoso- phy*, ed. D. J. O'Conner (New York: Free Press, 1964), p. 328.

[11]See D. P. Verene, *Hegel's Recollection: A Study of Images in The Phenomenology of Spirit* (Albany: State University of New York Press, 1985).

Geist may be translated either as "mind" or as "spirit," but neither is free of associations foreign to Hegel's meaning. "Mind," which Baillie prefers, is likely to suggest an individual mind; "spirit" is likely to suggest something ghostly; but neither suggestion is intended by Hegel's use of *Geist*. It is for him the fusion or synthesis of the mental and the physical—a reality that embodies an idea. Such a reality may be of one or another three basic types: subjective, objective, or absolute. An individual person, viewed as a self-conscious physical being—as a "rational animal," to use Aristotle's famous expression—is an example of "subjective" *Geist*. Institutions such as the family or the state, which are embodiments of social ideas, are examples of "objective" *Geist*. Art, religion, and philosophy, which are embodiments of the Absolute Idea, are the three forms of "absolute" *Geist*.

Aufhebung is a technical term of great importance to Hegel. In German it has numerous distinct and even contrary meanings, including "canceling," "overcoming," "transcending," "negating," "abolishing," "suppressing," "elevating," and "preserving." Hegel liked *Aufhebung* because of its dialectical implications. No single English word can convey the complexity that it held for him. As he employs it, *Aufhebung* connotes a development in which a new reality comes about thanks to a negating that is yet also a perfecting of its initial state of being, as when a child is at once negated and perfected by developing into an adult. In a sense the child is "abolished" in becoming an adult, and yet the child is also "preserved" in the adult. The adult is the result of the *Aufhebung* of the child: the child has been "canceled" yet "preserved" and "elevated" in the adult. The development from child to adult is a good illustration, borrowed from Hegel himself, of what he means by a dialectical process, and he constantly uses *Aufhebung* in describing such processes.

Begriff, usually translated as "notion" but sometimes as "concept," has roots similar to those of the English "comprehension." *Be(i)*, like "com," means "about;" *griff*, like "prehension," means "grasp." "A grip on," "the getting of a handle on," or simply "comprehension" are good renderings for *Begriff.* "Notion," however, is preferred by Baillie and has become the usual rendering for Hegel's *Begriff.* Unhappily, "notion" has the defect of suggesting a vague understanding or a feeling. The reader should bear in mind that "comprehension" is what is really meant, and for Hegel it principally means the comprehension of a dialectical relationship.

PARAGRAPH ANALYSIS

The following analysis is intended to outline the essential points of each paragraph of the Preface and Introduction to the *Phenomenology* as briefly and as clearly as possible. It is not intended as a running commentary upon either one.

Preface

1. The usual manner of introducing a philosophical work with a preface explaining its purpose, results, and historical circumstances is misleading. Philosophical truth cannot be expressed in this way.

2. Philosophy intends to bring together particularities, or separate factual elements, into a general idea or universality. Before this universal goal can be attained, it is necessary to treat each element as it would contribute to the whole. Hence the result of the philosophic enterprise can be understood only after the particulars have been comprehended in this whole. Philosophy cannot be analytically presented before this universality is reached.

3. The various philosophical systems are usually taken as expressing either "true" or "false" views, and one is expected to agree or disagree with any given system. Each system, however, contributes to the evolution of the truth. Philosophical systems are elements of an organic whole in which each is necessary to all the others and to the whole. It is therefore a mistake to suppose that some particular system would be

"true" in itself, apart from the whole, as if it and the other systems were not integrated into a whole.

4. To insist upon being told the results of a philosophical work or the earmarks that distinguish it from other works is a sure way *not* to acquire any substantive understanding of it. Results identified without considering how they were developed are scarcely intelligible, and merely to make comparisons is not to come to grips with the work in itself.

5. An acquaintance with general principles and points of view is only the beginning of enlightenment in any field. For depth of understanding we must really live with the subject matter, make it our own in details and nuances, and bring it into a reasoned system.

6. Philosophy by its very nature develops into science as its particular truths successively emerge and show themselves to be necessary elements in a system. Philosophical truth exists only in the form of intrinsically necessitated truth, as a system, which unfolds over the course of time.

7. Our assertion that philosophical truth is scientific in character runs counter to some contemporary schools of thought. They would maintain that truth is given in the form of an intuition or "feeling" that immediately grasps the Absolute, the very Being of God. In this view, truth is something first felt and then spoken, and not something reached by systematic conception.

8. A sense of *loss* is really at the bottom of this idea that truth is obtainable at once and without rigorous thought. This unhappy feeling has arisen because critical reflection has erased their previously unquestioned sense of the simple factuality of themselves and their world. Faced with this new and unwelcome thought, these disillusioned souls now call upon philosophy to restore their earlier feeling of undoubted *existence*. They wish consolation and edification rather than the hard truths of systematic philosophy.

9. This desire for consolation wishes philosophy to restore an earlier view in which divine matters were more important than the worldly, and things distant and eternal seemed more

real than the present. But now the opposite view pre-dominates—the world of experience draws most of our attention, and the spiritual is neglected.

10. Philosophic science appeals to neither of these views, but it must especially resist the temptation to cater to the many who only wish to enjoy vague sentiments about a vague divinity.

11. Those who rest in a complacent and unreflective emotional knowledge, and who pride themselves in "divine feelings," and of their feeling of the Divine, are always contemptuous of science and of the constraints of conceptual thinking. In their dreaming, these enthusiasts think themselves *above* science, but in fact they are *below* it, for their "insights" and prophecies are quite empty.

12. We are witnessing the dawn of a new epoch of progress. A long period of cultural gestation, of slow quantitative change, is about to give rise to a sudden qualitative change—a total revolution in our worldview. The old epoch is signaling its end by widespread frivolity, ennui, and foreboding.

13. Although a new worldview is upon us, as yet it exists only as a general and unspecified idea. From this general idea there will develop, slowly and with effort, all of the particular forms now latent within it. This new epoch will be fully understood only after all of the forms latent within it have been finally actualized.

14. When this new worldview first appears in outline, it seems to most people to be but an affair known by a few (esoteric). But before this science can become common intellectual property (exoteric), it must be explained in its connection to previous knowledge. Once this is accomplished, everyone will have access to the new science.

15. This new thought, as still undeveloped, is subjected to the critique of two groups, both of whom expect it to be presented in full detail. One group compares it unfavorably to older and so more detailed systems, which they (rightly) expect a science to emulate. The second group—advocates of "intuitive" knowledge—disparage the new science because

they disparage conceptual and systematic thought in general. In the course of time, the first group will find satisfaction in the new worldview.

16. Some members of the second group of critics (for example, the school of F. W. J. Schelling) believe that anything said to be new will turn out to be only an instance or illustration of some grand "principle" or "Absolute Idea," which they have already established and have at hand. These people cover whatever comes along under their "principle" and insist that it was always there. But their "absolute principle" is nothing more than a vague abstraction, which, rather than clarifying and distinguishing ideas, merely paints them over with the same color. This kind of busy but blurring activity is an intellectual "formalism" which, in applying the same formula to everything, obliterates all the detailed interrelationships of particular things and thoughts.

17. This empty formalism is said to give us the Absolute. It is maintained that within it, the Absolute, everything is One. All differences between things, all specifications, all contrasts are obliterated in this all-encompassing Absolute. Strictly speaking, the only truth that remains is the tautology that "the Absolute is the Absolute" ("A = A"). All particular truths disappear in the darkness of this one empty utterance. A philosophical night descends upon us in which only the Absolute can be seen—a "night in which all cows are black."

18. This confusing formalism will continue to attract people until someone clearly presents what is entailed in this "knowledge of absolute reality." Let us begin by first considering what such knowledge might be and some of the attitudes that would be opposed to such knowledge.

19. We begin by proposing that the Absolute ("the ultimate truth") is properly understood as both Subject and Substance. As Subject it is self-consciousness, self-reflective thought. As Substance, it is the *object* of thought, that which is known. The Absolute is both subject and object, thought, and its content. The full significance and meaning of this proposition will come only after we have developed our philosophical science,

but it can here be noted that previous thinkers have not taken the Absolute or God in this twofold manner, and so have been led into positing either one side or the other as primary.

20. The unity of Subject (thought) and Substance (object of thought) in the Absolute is not a given unity from the beginning. It is an *achieved* unity, realized in and through a *process*. True and living substance is a process, because it comes to be by existing *for itself*, and not because it is simply given. A "subject" first begins to exist for itself by becoming an object for itself. It achieves this by self-negation, by becoming an "other" to itself. This "other" first confronts the subject as an "object." Nevertheless, this opposite being, although "another" being, is merely the restatement and repositing of the first. In sum, subjective being is being that restates itself in the "other," which it itself has created. On the other hand, the "object" or Substance returns to its source in the subject when it is drawn back into thought, when it is known. Both Subject and Substance, in their activity of reflecting one another, create the Absolute.

21. The life of the Absolute (God as we seek to understand Him) might be described as an activity in which *love* discovers what it is by first projecting itself outward in the form of an "other" (a created world). This other is then drawn back lovingly into itself. However, such talk can easily fall into glib edification and sentimental preaching if it is forgotten that love also contains the notes of suffering and negativity. We cannot be satisfied if the Absolute, or God, is taken only "in itself," without any real relation to itself in its creation. Were this so, the Absolute would be devoid of self-consciousness, for self-consciousness depends upon an active relationship with another. An Absolute "per se" would be a mere abstract generality, an empty and unconscious "essence."

22. The Absolute is a *result* of its own activity. It is the outcome of a process of self-discovery by means of self-projection. In its first simple stage of being it is a mere unreflective generality or universal. Hence, to become fully itself, and so to exist *for itself*, it must develop its own specifications. This it

does by "negating itself," by opposing itself to itself as an "other" to itself. In the course of dealing with this "other," it finally comes into being for itself; it becomes self-conscious. Its coming into being for itself is thus "mediated" by (through the means of) the "other" that it has created out of itself. The truth of the Absolute, or "Absolute truth," encompasses the whole process—all of the self-mediating activity wherein the Absolute comes fully to itself by first projecting itself as Substance and then recovering itself as Subject.

23. This process whereby Absolute Subject is obtained by the loss of its given being, its initial existence, can appear as a negative process, unworthy of God. It is, however, a *positing* (positive) process that generates conscious self-identity or self-consciousness. Who would deny these perfections of subjectivity to God? The goal and purpose of all of the self-negating activity in which the Absolute has gone out of itself into an "other" will be its self-conscious freedom. At the end it will exist for itself and be at one with itself.

24. What is here to be understood, despite the present disregard of purposive, end-directed action, is that reason acts with purpose. Reason is the act of a self-conscious and self-moving Subject; it is both the principle cause of life and the end of life. Reason, in action, is the restless unfolding of the self; and in itself it is identical with the essence of the self. The initial life of reason, which is simple self-identity and self-reference, recovers itself in the end. Reason is both the source and the goal of all activity.

25. It will not do to simply assert that the Absolute is "subject" and let it go at that. To mean by such an assertion that the Absolute, as subject, is not a static "thing," does not really help us to comprehend the meaning of subjectivity. To merely employ, without any further thought about them, such terms as "Absolute," "God," or "moral order of the world" is a waste of time, as they lose all significance. Indeed, in such unreflective use of these terms they are not only rendered meaningless, but it even becomes impossible to give them a meaning. Their full significance must be developed.

26. Knowledge is completed and realized only in the form of a science or system. Knowledge is not a premise but a result. The beginning statements or principles of any philosophy cannot be said to be completely true, for they need to be fully exposed, criticized, and finally refuted as not being true knowledge insofar as they are only a beginning. Initial knowledge is incomplete; however, it can rise up through its own self-criticism into complete and true knowledge.

27. The highest conception of all is that the "Absolute is Spirit [*Geist*]." The Absolute, as essentially active and creative, has set itself apart from itself in what we call the "world," and by this creative act it has become an object for itself. From our point of view the Absolute is said to exist as both creator and in its creation. In order for it, however, to come into the fullness of its being, it must know itself as being in its creation; it must become self-conscious. Absolute mind is spirit that knows itself as its own object, as its own creation. This absolute self-knowledge is [*Wissenschaft*]. Science is reason knowing itself. Science is the reasonable mind that finds itself at home in the world; and it is the hidden reason of the world, as its laws and truths, which finds expression in the scientific mind.

28. Science is expected to help reason arrive at an understanding of itself not only as something in itself but as something for itself—as something existing in the world. The unscientific or unreasonable mind cannot grasp the reason that is expressed in the world, and so finds itself in an alien world. Because science maintains that the world is reasonable, this isolated mind condemns science. In isolating itself from the reason present in the world, this mind takes only its own dogmas and certitudes as true. But it yet remains confounded by the world and is always tempted to fall into the "unreasonable" world. This alienated mind faces the dilemma of choosing between its "unworldly" (heavenly) certitudes or of falling into the uncertain experiences of the world. But although this sort of mind sees no possible reconciliation between the ideal world (the world of mind) and the world of experience (na-

ture), the scientific mind grasps the notion that the two worlds are complementary expression of the Absolute.

29. A long and difficult journey must be taken by the mind in order to reach absolute knowledge. The *Phenomenology* sets forth the stages of this journey in which science evolves. The path is not that which is commonly imagined; this knowledge that absolute reason is expressed in both mind and nature comes gradually to the mind, and not as a sudden inspiration— "as if fired from a pistol."

30. This journey is the same for an individual as it has been for humankind. An individual, when advancing to higher levels of consciousness and knowledge, passes the very same stages or shapes of consciousness that humankind has passed through in its history. In recapitulating general history, an individual unthinkingly assimilates a cultural heritage, such as a definite language. But science understands that this same cultural material, unconsciously known and used by individuals, is actually the fundamental instrument through which the Absolute comes into self-consciousness. The successive historical cultures have been the creatures of absolute reason, its instruments through which it finds self-consciousness. They are not merely things "given" to individuals at different times and places.

31. Every stage and shape through which human consciousness has passed was necessary. The universal mind, *Weltgeist*, has always expressed itself in a manner that can be understood by the scientific individuals of its era. But in order to reach this level of absolute knowing, the individual must fully know each of the earlier stages of universal mind. Only after this careful analysis of all previous stages of thought will these prior cultures be properly grasped as the true and necessary premises of the present age.

32. The thought-forms (or culture) of most individuals are usually left unquestioned, as things so "well known" that they are unconsciously accepted. But as it is the concern of science to know the universal mind, then reason will bring these things out into the open and question them.

33. What is "familiar" is by that very reason *not* properly known, for it is uncritically and superficially taken up as a fixed and valid point from which to begin and end thinking.

34. Understanding is the analysis of a familiar idea by the process of breaking it up into its elements. But to break up anything is a negative act. Hence the understanding is a negative power; it separates that which appeared as a living unity into dead parts. But the life of mind or purposive reason does not fear death, and so it proceeds to drive the analytic understanding to its ultimate limit. Only by so doing is negation transformed into affirmation. The given and familiar must be broken; its simple unity destroyed, but only so that in the end it be truly understood as a living unity of many elements—an organism.

35. Ancient thinkers directed their attention to educating the "natural" (unphilosophical) minds of their contemporaries. They endeavored to do this by drawing out or abstracting the universal meanings or ideas latent in commonplace thinking. Such is our cultural heritage from the ancients that today virtually everyone is only too familiar with these universal ideas, which now have petrified into lifeless formulations. The modern mind has a modern task: to stop controlling and manipulating these unexamined certitudes and fixed definitions. By so permitting them to work out their own inner logic, they will become "what they are in truth" and not what we would make of them.

36. Scientific progress is obtained by allowing ideas (as "spiritual entities") to unfold their own meaning and purpose. They will follow their own necessity toward the formation of a systematic whole. Knowledge evolves, not by chance reflections or by the application of a formal logic upon some already established material, but by the self-movement of thought itself. This self-movement will, in its progress, finally encompass the whole of our experience.

37. The *Phenomenology*, in a systematic manner, will begin by examining unreflective thought or mind (mind "in its immediate aspect").

38. All consciousness, however reflective or unreflective, involves a distinction between a subject that thinks and the object being thought. Over the course of intellectual history, there has been an evolving relationship between subject and object, and this can be called "experience." This evolution has expressed itself in the various forms of human culture, each of which can serve as a record from which a history of the experiences of consciousness can be recapitulated. This *Phenomenology*, as the scientific exposition of this history of consciousness, will focus upon the Absolute as both the source and the end of this history, and will understand this history as the process of absolute reason, or "Mind [*Geist*]." Our exposition will recount the experiences of Mind from its first simple and primitive existence, through the periods of its self-generated alienation, until it reaches an absolute end. The task of our *Phenomenology* will end when it has comprehended all the stages of knowledge that have lead Mind to its completion as Absolute Subject.

39. It is usually imagined that there is something defective or negative about the radical separation that exists between thought and its object (or between ego and nonego). However, were it not for this "negative" relationship, there could be no such thing as a living subject. There can be no life whatsoever without opposition and difference; there can be no interaction—only dead repetition. It was to become alive that Absolute substance, as Mind, created the division of subject and object out of its own substance, for it was only by such a division that it could come to know itself, to be "for itself." By its act of self-division it created itself as a living subject, and has come to know itself as absolute, as that which encompasses both subject and object. True logic (or speculative philosophy) can only begin after our *Phenomenology* is completed, for only then can the full content or "moments" of the consummated Mind be presented in proper form—as "truth in the form of truth."

40. Why should we not go straight to logic ("the science of ultimate truth") in the first place? Why must we first recapitu-

late in a "phenomenology" the many stages of untruths or half-truths that have had to be "negated" as Mind progressed to the ultimate truth? The answer lies in a clearer idea of the role that "negating" or "negativity" plays in relation to ultimate truth.

41. True and false, just as subject and object, have no real significance apart from one another. The truth is not something simply given, already prepared for use apart from any previous consideration of the false. The opposition between the two is an essential stage in knowing. True ideas are arrived at by the mind passing through (negating, cancelling) stages of lesser truths or "untruths," in which the greater truths are consciously understood as containing the premises of lesser truths. These lesser truths are harmoniously preserved as previous stages of the final truths.

42. Dogmatic minds believe that truth is some sort of a "given" that can be presented in unqualified and fixed terms. These dogmatic truths are considered to be absolutely isolated from anything untrue. But such assertions have little to do with philosophical truth.

43. Historical facts such as "Caesar was born in 100 B.C." have no rational necessity about them, for they are contingent and conditional events. But the historian must be rational, for past experience needs to be investigated and evaluated. Reason is present when any given "fact" is drawn forth from the mass of transient experience. It is only reason that uncovers these "facts" and gives them value and meaning.

44. It might seem to some that reason is fully exercised in mathematics. But a mathematical "proof" (the form of mathematical reasoning) only serves to implement a particular end for the mathematician and has no utility or significance beyond that. Proofs serve only to link intentions and results, and once the desired goal is reached, they lose their usefulness and are discarded. Philosophical reasoning is also used to come to a result, but unlike mathematics, this result will essentially contain all of the principles, premises, and logic that have caused its existence.

45. Mathematical knowledge is analytic and deals with the external features of its objects. For example, in geometry a triangle is broken down into parts that are common to other geometrical figures, and then, after this deconstruction, it is once again reconstructed from these common elements. This negation and breaking down of the whole into elements shared by other figures might be seen as negating or "falsifying" the "truth," i.e., the original unity of a triangle. A similar kind of "falsifying" occurs in philosophical thinking when separate ideas are synthesized into a higher and more comprehensive idea (a notion, *Begriff*). In this process the particular features making this or that separate idea only *partially* true are negated or falsified.

46. For the mathematician, there is no inner logic or necessity to be found within mathematical objects (numbers or figures). In geometry, for example, reason is applied from without upon the various figures (point, line, etc.) and not seen as inherent within the figures themselves. Hence, geometrical operations are imposed upon the figures and are not considered to be prescribed by the nature of the figures themselves. Geometricians proceed by simply proposing various constructions of geometrical figures; by so doing they hope to arrive at a general truth (theorem). Their proofs begin as trials, as possible ways that might generate a desired result. The successful proof is valued only for its utility, for supporting a theorem—and once it is successful it is no longer useful and so can be discarded.

47. Mathematics—that is, "pure" mathematics—deals with quantitative abstractions, with geometrical properties of figures or arithmetic properties of units, none of which are objects of concrete experience. A knowledge of such empty and unessential abstractions cannot concern philosophy. Mathematics advances only by the principle of equality, of equations and comparisons; it relies upon such dry principles as "things equal to the same thing are equal to one another." It does not enter into living activity, but rather manipulates, from without, various formulas of identity and nonidentity.

Philosophical thinking grasps the inner meaning of concepts in the course of their own self-generating relationships. Mathematics, on the contrary, is unable even to comprehend the real significance (intrinsic relationships) of such realities as number, infinity, space, and time.

48. It is true that "applied" mathematics, as opposed to "pure," does indeed treat some aspects of concrete experience, for example, certain physical relationships occurring in actual time and space. However, in applied mathematics, the event or "fact" that is to be mathematically considered has been taken up as something that is simply "given." The event itself is not questioned as to its sources or the ground of its existence. The given event is taken up only as data to be analyzed and presented in mathematical form. Because they do not touch upon the nature of their objects, the "proofs" of applied mathematics will tell us nothing profound about our world. For example, nothing at all is learned about the real nature of time or space in themselves from being acquainted with Archimedes' proofs concerning the principles of the lever.

49. Since mathematics deals only in numbers and figures, it is only able to represent the movement of time as a deadening linear repetition of fixed units. Limited to working with standardized abstractions of measure and relation, mathematics cannot express the dynamic self-movement and passing away of time.

50. Philosophy concerns itself with concrete realities, not with empty abstractions. It understands reality in terms of self-generating activity that appears now in one form and later in another, continuously moving. What endures through all the coming and going of reality's forms or appearances is just the process itself. This is the whole of what exists; it is reality itself. Each of the stages of the process is as positive and necessary as it is negative and transient. Past stages, as preserved in memory, may be recalled into existence by the mind's activity of self-recollection. Past activity exists only in present knowledge.

51. Logic, as we now will use the term, is the systematic exposition of the process in which truth and reality make their appearance. This is not "logic" in the traditional sense, which tries to imitate mathematics by sundry "proofs" and "disproofs" of theoremlike propositions. Today, we have tired of this quasi-mathematics and can no longer accept it as a way to the truth. Logic, as this way, is not imported into philosophy from mathematics or some other discipline, but is itself an essentially philosophical enterprise that exposes the manner in which "truth moves itself by its very nature."

52. But in our dismissal of the mechanical ordering of traditional logic, we must take care not to fall into an opposite frame of mind—one that turns from order and method to incoherent "inspiration" and "prophecy." True logic and method will follow the systematic and necessary elaboration of ideas.

53. The triadic method of thinking that Kant discussed, wherein we proceed from thesis, to antithesis, to synthesis, may represent the right method of science. However, it has been much abused. It has inspired people to imagine that "syntheses" are possible between all manner of things, between east and west, subjectivity and objectivity, plus and minus, male and female, etc., etc.

54. Such a formalistic imposition of any pregiven "plan" or "method" is called "construction." By gathering together and classifying all sorts of things under some triadic schema, the elements are given an appearance of unity, as if they shared in some idea. This facile ordering by labeling is often admired but has no scientific value whatsoever. As discussed in paragraph 17, the final result of such mechanical gathering of lifeless data is contempt for such empty activity and a turn to a mysticism that dissolves everything into an Absolute.

55. That the schema of thesis-antithesis-synthesis has been misused should not cause surprise, because the excellent is always recognized, if not understood. Excellence is obtained when an idea has been fully developed, and so in this development we should expect some aberration.

56. Science will develop into a unitary system through the purposive action of reason (the notion). This activity begins with an apparently simple universal or generality (a thesis), which then proceeds to unfold its inner content by generating its own opposition (an antithesis) to itself. The process concludes (with a synthesis). In this, the original universal "takes this evolved content [the opposite] . . . back into itself" and by so doing develops itself into a self-reflective and conceptually explicit universal. The unreflective simplicity of the original thesis has developed itself into a fully explicit and self-reflective concept. What has happened in this process is not predetermined by something outside the process; it happens by virtue of "the self-directing inner soul of the concrete content" of the apparently simple thesis. "Understanding" (*Verstand*), as we use the term, is a kind of thinking that simply cannot appreciate what is going on in such a process. From the point of view of understanding, all ideas have sharp edges, fixed meanings, and may be neatly classified; there can be no question of an idea's evolving into an opposite idea and then somehow reabsorbing it to generate a superior synthesis of them both.

57. Understanding looks at everything from an external point of view. It likes to place a precise label and give an exact name to whatever it encounters. It does not "enter into the inherent content" of anything but stays on the surface of what it considers. Genuine reason, or true science, does not stand outside of its object in an attempt to "survey," but rather enters into it and "abandons" itself to the subject matter. Only after the inner content of the subject matter has unfolded itself will reason come "back to itself" by making that content its own, and by placing it within the context of the whole truth elevate this limited content into a "higher truth."

58. A substance is something that is self-identical to itself and that exists in itself as a self-supporting thing. But substance is implicitly a subject. This is so because "self-identity" is an abstraction, something that is thought of when one thinks of substance. But thought is subjectivity. Hence, the conception

of substance entails the conception of subject. Further, anything is defined to be what it is because of its quality. But to be
something distinctive is to be a substance, to be for oneself.
But being that is for or with itself is essentially what is meant
by thought.

59. In other words, "being is thought," for "being" connotes that which exists in itself ("substance"), which, at the
same time, has turned out to be a something thought (an
abstraction). If we take substance as being that is *known* or as
it exists in abstract thought for itself, then its subsistence has
been divided. Being is then both identical with itself and
abstracted from itself. It exists then not as simple being but as a
process of becoming in which it subsists both in itself and as
the abstraction of itself ("for itself").

60. As being is thought, so thought cannot treat of its
object (being), as if it was something totally different than
thought—as we find in that self-certain dogmatism that thinks
only of its own thoughts. True science, which does not separate thought and being, is integrated with the movement of its
object. Knowing is deeply at one with its object and is caught
up in its activity. This involvement in objective reality means
that real knowing will lose its purely inward and private
character.

61. As we have seen, from the standpoint of understanding
existence, or substance, is taken up as a fixed and determinate
thought. Substance is first understood as Anaxagoras thought:
"Mind" or νοῦς. Later, with Plato, it became more definitely an
"Idea," which means only "species" or "kind." But today
such simple terms are not valued as sufficiently edifying to
apply to such grand thoughts as the beautiful or the holy, and
so other terms are employed, although they actually obscure
the matter at hand.

62. However, although the idea that understanding has of
existence is simply that it is a fixed and self-identical being, a
simple static thing (a given), this idea nevertheless contains the
seed of its own self-dissolution. The negation of this fixed idea
does not come from without, but is born of its own inner life.

Understanding cannot be separated from the dynamics of thought, and its fixed ideas will be caught up and transformed in the process of reason.

63. The whole of reality, we find, consists in rational activity, in dynamic interaction between knowing and the object known. This rational activity is the true realm of theory and speculative thought. By its own action the object known develops itself into a definite quality, a meaning (an idea), and thereby into a logical form of thought (reason). Being (object) coincides with being thought (idea) in the reasoning (thinking) process. The logical forms of thought are not imposed upon reality but rather naturally and necessarily (dialectically) emerge from it.

64. A systematic expression of our philosophical method would be given in a fully developed speculative philosophy. The present *Phenomenology*, however, attempts nothing more than a preliminary and incomplete exposition of the method, as would-be critics of this book should bear in mind.

65. As an unfamiliar work, the *Phenomenology* will naturally be opposed by those who feel that their own viewpoints are threatened by it, and who think there is nothing new to learn. On the other hand, there are those who, like ultra-revolutionaries in politics, enjoy displaying their personal freedom by welcoming anything out of the ordinary.

66. True students of science, however, must soberly devote themselves to the hard work of conceptual thinking and attend to the basic elements and functions of science. They must avoid either thinking in terms of imaginative pictures (*Vorstellungen*) or in terms of abstract generalities. In the former there is content without form, in the latter form without content. Scientific thought is thought that enters into the self-generating process of reality itself, and that recognizes itself within that movement.

67. Self-centered "reasoning" that gives itself over to debating and arguing, and likes to adopt a skeptical and "negative" tone, will, of course, look askance at what we have identified as conceptual thought. This negative attitude will

always avoid direct engagement with its subject matter, which it considers as something foreign to it. Caught up in its own denials, this empty skepticism cannot come to appreciate the real way in which "negativity," as a stage within the process of thought, actually generates *positive* results.

68. Understanding (*Verstand*) rejects the idea that thought itself can contribute anything to the matter under consideration. Reason, however, knows that the thinking subject is actively involved in the development of its object. In the eyes of reason, the object of thought *evolves*, and reason sees thought as integrated into that process. In this view, the evolving content is not just something said or predicated as an event happening outside of the thinking subject, but as an event involving the subject. Insofar as this evolution is not independent of thinking, its movement of reason will be thoughtful, and imaginative thinking (*vorstellen*) will be held back from falling into nonsense.

69. At first, the thinking subject usually takes itself to be something with a fixed identity, as something that exists apart from what it thinks about. But it will find that it is not really independent of them when it comes to reflect that, as a knowing ego, it actively *orders* (combines in thought the predicates or qualities of) what it is thinking. With this insight, the thinking subject realizes that it has become part of what it knows, and has evolved. For this reason, it will come to know that it will be impossible for it to return to its state prior to that knowing.

70. Formally expressed, reason, or the "speculative judgment," overcomes the sharp distinction between subject and predicate in the judgments of understanding. Reason is analogous to rhythm in polyphonic music, which combines two or more independent melodies into one harmonious composition without altering their individual identities. Reason links subject and predicate in such a manner that both are seen to require one another. For example, whereas the understanding might make the judgment that "Thinkers are not the objects they think about," reason would grasp that the subject

"thinkers" requires the predicate "objects they think about," and *vice-versa*.

71. As an example, consider the proposition "God is Being." The predicate ("Being") signifies the class that contains the subject ("God"). As containing ("absorbing") the fundamental meaning of "God," the predicate "Being" is now also identified with its subject. The subject has been taken up or assimilated into the universal class of the predicate. "God," in short, can be found in "Being." On the other hand, "Being" is also found in "God." The two terms, as reflecting one another, are not separated but exist in harmonious relation.

72. In another example, consider the proposition "the real is the universal." In this, the subject "real" is understood as being a member in the class of the predicate "universal." The subject has lost its fixed and separate character by sharing in the meaning of the predicate. It is no longer possible to think adequately of the subject by itself; it must henceforth be viewed as carrying the meaning of the predicate as well.

73. The complication that this way of reasoning places upon our use of language makes it difficult to present simple and unconditioned statements. The inherent complexity that philosophy detects between subject and predicate is the cause of those complaints, heard even from intelligent people, that philosophical writings are not easily understood. Philosophical writings must be read again and again, since by exposing usually hidden relationships between subjects and predicates they compel us to rethink what we have (up to then) taken as granted.

74. We must try to avoid mixing up common or ordinary ways of thinking ("ratiocination") with the philosophical. The former, as nonspeculative, merely attaches a predicate to a subject without dealing with its inner or conceptual relationship to that subject. These two ways of thinking are incompatible, and should be kept separate.

75. Nonspeculative thought has its place, as things can be predicated of subjects without necessarily looking at the inner process that links subjects and predicates. However, specula-

tive thought consciously attends to and openly states the process by which a subject term returns or reflects back upon itself from out of what has been said (predicated) of it. This process, by which a subject is first found "outside" of itself in a predicate and then is seen to have obtained a higher meaning by its restatement within that predicate, is dialectical in nature. Speculative truth will express this process, which is neither a "proof" nor a "demonstration" of the meaning of a subject. With speculative thought predicates are not pasted like labels upon subjects, without any fundamental connection to them, but understood and stated as the necessary result of the inner process of their subjects, as containing the "higher" truth of their subjects.

76. Of course, propositions as ordinarily expressed occur in speculative philosophy—distinctive subjects and predicates must be used. However, the subjects of these propositions do not acquire speculative meaning by having predicates *attached* to them, a matter of "external knowledge." Speculative knowledge arises from the implicit nature of the subject itself, and propositions that appear in philosophy are only starting points for dialectical development; in themselves they are only empty forms pointing toward the truth.

77. The name "God" is best avoided in speculative philosophy, as "God" is usually understood as a static and fixed subject without any relation to an object or without a predicate. "God" is not understood as a speculative concept capable of self-development. Such a term, when thus taken as indifferent and alien to any real content, will become the subject of empty predicates, of vapid edification; anything can be said of this "God." Philosophy must consider its subjects as inherently active conceptions.

78. In everyday life, a good deal of training and preparation is considered prerequisite for beginning serious work in science or art, but not so in philosophy. In the popular mind, everyone can easily set about doing philosophy by the use of their own "natural reason." Further, philosophy is usually taken (or mistaken) as empty thinking without any "real"

objects in mind. But the fact is, however, that no truth or significance whatsoever can be sustained unless based upon a philosophical foundation.

79. There are those who, seeking an easy shortcut to knowledge, look to divine revelations or plain "healthy common sense" as suitable substitutes for philosophy. These crude and uncultivated thinkers even dare to see themselves as "inspired by genius," but they produce neither poetry nor philosophy, only trivialities and disorder.

80. When this sort of "common sense" dabbles in philosophy, its shallow insights are said to be truths coming up from "deep down in its own heart." But when critical reason dares to probe into these deeply felt "truths," it is rebuked as being but "sophistry" or "visionary dreaming." Feeling, or "the oracle within," is the unquestionable standard of common sense by which everything is judged. But if inarticulate inner feeling would replace open thought, then animality would prevail over humanity, and the only community proper to humanity, the "community of conscious life," would disintegrate into a collection of dumb brutes.

81. True thoughts and scientific insights are given neither in commonplace observations nor in flashes of genius. They are reached only by the hard mental work of critical thinking. Only conceptual rigor can bring truth into the universal form available to every self-conscious reason.

82. Since the scientific character of a philosophy is valued today, we may hope that our attempt to systematically present and justify science as a conceptual process will be accepted. In any case, the truth has a way of being recognized when its time is ripe and the public is prepared. Indeed, the public is more inclined to take a more open and receptive view of a new philosophy than those who would act as the representatives of philosophy. The truth will prevail.

83. The contribution must needs be small that any one person can make toward the further development of the whole of truth. Because of this, individual self-interest must be forgotten, as science itself requires. The person who does this

will be doing all that can be done—no more can or should be expected.

Introduction

1. Before beginning to philosophize, it seems quite reasonable to engage in a testing and evaluation of knowledge itself, as this seems to be the instrument used to obtain the truth.
2. But if knowledge is understood as some sort of an instrument that apprehends reality, then by its own act it would in some way modify or disturb reality as it exists in itself (the Absolute). But then how could we ever know reality as it is in itself? If, on the other hand, we assume knowledge to be some sort of a passive medium that does not in any way disturb reality in itself, we are nevertheless still separated from reality by that very "medium." Once again, could we ever know reality as it is in itself? But all such testing and evaluation of knowledge, natural as they might at first seem, are only pointless exercises; they rest upon the false premise that knowledge is a potential means to the truth rather than the actual presence of the truth. If we have the ability to detect and discount distorting influences upon our knowledge, then we must already have accurately apprehended reality.
3. The fear of error that distrusts science rests upon the unexamined presupposition that knowledge is an instrument or medium. It then follows that the knowers and their knowledge, although accepted as realities, are nevertheless separated from the real (the Absolute). Such fear of error, which sets knowledge apart from truth and reality, is rather a fear of the truth.
4. But although it is a fact that only the Absolute is true, or that only the True is absolute, it is nevertheless possible to set this fact aside by pointing to relative truths that can satisfy general knowledge. However, to continue this sort of idle talk, without first examining the meanings of such terms as "absolute" and "knowledge," can only lead us to confusing the distinction between absolute and relative truths.

5. But we need not concern ourselves any further with these foolish questions dealing with the many purported relationships that might hold between knowledge and reality. It seems evident that those who do engage in this initial and ongoing distrust of science do so only to avoid its hard work. These busy questioners, who display a great deal of seriousness about the "possibility" of science, are actually evading science by not really examining the "familiar" concepts they talk about. However, this show of knowledge, which tries to avoid science, will quickly vanish when science makes its appearance.

6. Science does not "come on the scene" suddenly. Like all other phenomena, it makes a gradual appearance. Nevertheless, science will eventually free itself completely from being confused with other ways of knowing, ways that are historically conditioned, and will show itself to be *more* than just another way of knowing. This will be accomplished, not by us, but by science itself through its own self-development. It will be seen to be self-justifying. But for the moment, since science is only making its first appearance, it must be treated as but another phenomena. Like other appearances of knowledge in general, it cannot at first make any claim to be more than an appearance, a phenomena. The history of how science appears and attains completeness is recorded in this *Phenomenology*.

7. Our record or exposition of ordinary knowledge on its way to science, to the completed notion, is not itself science. It is a record. It can be taken as either the illustration of how natural consciousness historically evolves into true knowledge, or how the soul carries out, in successive embodiments, its own inner program, a program that directs it toward a clear self-consciousness of what it is in itself.

8. Natural and everyday thinking is initially confident that it represents nothing less than true and completed knowledge, and would claim final authority on all matters dealing with truth or falsity. Any questioning that would cast doubt upon its natural role is viewed as a threat to its very existence. It looks

upon the path leading to true knowledge as one upon which it will become totally insignificant, upon which it will collapse into skepticism. But what this commonplace knowing has yet to grasp is that even what it considers "skepticism" (a questioning of everything from its own unquestioned standpoint) is not at all the skepticism found on the path to science. Scientific skepticism is unlimited, a total and all-encompassing skepticism that treats all apparent (or phenomenal) knowledge as "untruth" or unrealized truth.

9. The road to scientific knowledge is not a given, a sort of ready-made map that one must simply follow, but is a process that engages the mind in the course of its own self-development. This process requires more than a simple confidence and "conviction" that one is correct, but rather demands a radical skepticism "directed to the whole compass of phenomenal knowledge." Such insight into the "untruth" of such knowledge is the condition sine qua non for the testing of truth. Ordinary thinking should surrender its unexamined certitudes and question its prejudices and dogmas, for otherwise it will remain forever incapable of self-development.

10. The *Phenomenology* will show that knowledge is engaged in a necessary progress as it advances from one viewpoint or form of thought to another. Its advance will always be characterized by a skeptical rejection of past forms as "untruths." Nevertheless, it must be noted that this process of rejection is not merely a denial—a process resulting in "nothing." This is what the unreflective ("one-sided") skeptic thinks to be the case. On the contrary, it always happens that if something in particular is denied, then, as a consequence, something else is implied. In the skeptical rejection of a particular "untruth," a new truth will come about, not "nothing" but rather what is implied in the denial of the inadequate truth. The denial has generated a particular and positive result, a "determinate nothing" *possessing a definite content*. The mind's dissatisfaction and rejection of partial truths provoke its advance toward complete truth.

11. The goal of knowledge, just as the path that leads to it, is fixed and necessitated. Final knowledge is reached only when the mind, having overcome and assimilated all of its past untrue forms, comes into complete self-consciousness and self-confidence. Until it reaches its goal, the mind will be driven by its own inner discontent to go "beyond itself" and to reach restlessly forward for ever higher truths. Our mind can find no secure rest in itself until it completes itself and is no longer driven to a "beyond." Those who attempt to avoid this discomforting path by lazy refusals to think, or easy slogans, or clever arguments will find no comfort; such rationalizations lead only to alienation and bitterness.

12. It yet remains for us to consider the method of evaluation to be employed in our *Phenomenology*. We are immediately confronted with a question: if we are to evaluate the merits of the various types of knowledge that occur before we reach the final level of science, then what can we use as a measure? It seems reasonable to maintain that only science itself, as an absolute knowledge, could serve as our standard. But we have hardly sketched out its concept, let alone justified it as absolute knowledge. Besides, the justification of science as absolute knowledge is the main intention of our *Phenomenology*. How then can we use science to test other forms of knowledge without first having tested science? Given this objection, how is it logically possible to proceed any further in this study?

13. As we earlier pointed out, it is natural for consciousness (mind) to first set itself apart from its objects and to establish definitions of knowledge and truth that involve complex relations between itself and the objects it has set from itself. What real meaning might be found in these distinctions and relationships is not something we should get involved in at this time. This will all come out in the course of our inquiry. However, what is important at this time is that we should simply take up, *as they appear to us*, the things presented by consciousness. We will not begin by analyzing and question-

ing the immediate data of consciousness, but we will begin by
accepting these determinations of our natural consciousness
as simple facts.

14. However, insofar as we take knowledge to be the principal object of our examination and try to find out what it is
"in itself" (*Ansich*), it paradoxically follows that we really
cannot deal with it "in itself," but only as it appears "for us."
How, then, is it ever possible to discover what it really is "in
itself"? All of our judgments regarding whether or not this or
that way of knowing is true or not would only be our decision,
based upon our knowledge. And so, since the standard of what
is to be held true or not would only be subjective, only a
matter of how it appears to us, then our judgments could
always be discounted.

15. But these objections all vanish when we realize that our
examination of knowledge does not accept, as ultimate, the
natural viewpoint that absolutely separates thought from its
object (or completely distinguishes the "in itself" from the
"for itself"). The central object we examine is simply consciousness itself, and consciousness transcends and encompasses all of the distinctions introduced and presupposed by
natural knowledge. Consciousness is the universal field in
which all distinctions of thought naturally occur, and it alone
is in the position to absolutely determine the relative degree of
correspondence between any thought or notion (*Begriff*) and
an object ("being"). Consciousness, in so comprehending the
compatibility of notion and object, will thereby be the criterion of truth.

16. We cannot add anything to the activity of our self-examining consciousness, and to rightly examine the various
forms of knowledge we need "simply and solely to look on."
These forms are but the forms of consciousness itself, and
within it objects are distinguished as either being "in themselves" or "for" consciousness. In the course of its activity,
consciousness will alter what it has established as knowledge
when its thought does not correspond to the object. In so
doing, the object or being is altered for consciousness. Con-

sciousness will always try to bring about a compatibility within itself between the apparent subject and object that has been introduced into it by the act of natural thought. However, if consciousness cannot ultimately bring about an equation between them, then it will change its perspective, and a new criteria for determining the identification of subjective thought and its object will come into being. Hence, the *Phenomenology* will be an examination not only of what we know but how we know it to be so, of knowledge and the standard of knowledge.

17. "Experience" is the process of alteration just described. It arises out of the interaction occurring in the field of consciousness between thought and its object, between knower and known. In the course of its alteration, consciousness discovers that what it has been treating as but an external object per se is in fact only another perspective of consciousness itself; in other words, an "experience." This new product is the resultant of the external object's own negation of itself as a merely external object. It then becomes, for consciousness, the experienced truth or the "essential reality" of the object per se.

18. "Experience," we admit, is usually understood in a quite different sense than we have proposed. It commonly means a mental process in which our knowledge of something is increased by seeing it in some way related to another object. In this view, experience is treated as a continuing display of more or less chance encounters between objective (per se) entities. But for *us*, this "experience," taken in this everyday sense and along with the whole outlook it involves, will *itself* fall under *our* viewpoint, and so become *our* "experience." This new way of looking at ordinary experience will be "our doing." Here, when observing human experience, we will see that it is not merely an ongoing and random collection of events that happen to occur in consciousness, but the necessitated progress of mind itself. We will observe the logic that operates, as it were, "behind the back" of natural consciousness, and show how it brings consciousness to ever higher

levels of completion. This necessitated progression of the mind's experience is for *us* the object per se.

19. If this progression were not necessitated, then neither our *Phenomenology* nor the pathway that leads to it could be called "scientific." Science is the revelation of necessity.

20. We shall see that consciousness, as its experience grows, will take in more and more of reality until, in the end, it will fully experience itself. It will become totally self-comprehending. Everything that natural consciousness had at first experienced as an alien "other," as a pure "object," will be grasped in this ultimate science as but an aspect, a "moment," within consciousness itself. At the level of absolute knowledge consciousness will experience its own essence as the systematic whole in which all reality is rationally encompassed.

A SELECTIVE BIBLIOGRAPHY OF TRANSLATIONS AND STUDIES IN ENGLISH

I. Hegel Translations

Aesthetics. 2 vols. Translated by T. M. Knox. Oxford: Clarendon Press, 1975.

Berlin Phenomenology. Translated from the *Encyclopaedia of the Philosophical Sciences* by M. J. Petry. Dordrecht, Holland: D. Reidel, 1981.

Christian Religion. Translated by Peter C. Hodgson. Missoula, MT: Scholars Press, 1979.

Difference between Fichte and Schelling. Translated by H. S. Harris and W. Cerf. Albany: State University of New York Press, 1977.

Difference between the Fichtean and Schellingian Systems of Philosophy. Translated by Jere P. Surber. Atascadero, CA: Ridgeview Press, 1981.

Early Theological Writings. Translated by T. M. Knox. Philadelphia: University of Pennsylvania Press, 1976; reprint, Chicago: University of Chicago Press, 1984.

Encyclopedia of Philosophy. Abridged and translated by Gustav E. Mueller. New York: Philosophical Library, 1959.

Faith and Knowledge. Translated by W. Cerf and H. S. Harris. Albany: State University of New York Press, 1977.

Hegel: The Letters. Translated by Clark Butler and Christiane Seiler. Bloomington: Indiana University Press, 1984.

Hegel and the Human Spirit: A Translation of the Jena Lectures on the Philosophy of Spirit (1805–6) with Commentary. Translated by Leo Rauch. Detroit: Wayne State University Press, 1983.

The Introduction to Hegel's Philosophy of Fine Art. Translated by B. Bosanquet. London: Routledge and Kegan Paul, 1905.

Introduction to the Lectures on the History of Philosophy. Translated by T.M. Knox and A.V. Miller. Oxford: Clarendon Press, 1987.

Introduction to The Philosophy of History. Translated by Leo Rauch. Indianapolis: Hackett Publishing Co., 1988.

The Jena System, 1804–5: Logic and Metaphysics. Translated by John W. Burbidge and George di Giovanni. Buffalo: McGill-Queens University Press, 1987.

Lectures on the History of Philosophy. 3 vols. Translated by E. S. Haldane. London: Kegan Paul, 1892; reprint, London: Routledge and Kegan Paul, 1955; reprint, Atlantic Highlands, NJ: Humanities Press, 1983.

Lectures on the Philosophy of World History: Introduction. Translated by H. B. Nisbet. Cambridge: Cambridge University Press, 1975.

Lectures on the Philosophy of World History: Reason in History. Translated by D. Forbes and H. B. Nisbet. Cambridge: Cambridge University Press, 1981.

Lectures on the Philosophy of Religion. 3 vols. Translated by E. B. Speirs and J. B. Sanderson. London: Routledge and Kegan Paul, 1895; reprint, Atlantic Highlands, NJ: Humanities Press, 1968.

Lectures on the Philosophy of Religion: Vol. I, *The Concept of Religion* (1984); Vol. II, *Determinate Religion* (1987); Vol. III, *The Consummate Religion* (1985). Edited by Peter C. Hodgson, translated by Robert F. Brown, et al. Berkeley: University of California Press.

Lectures on the Philosophy of Religion: One Volume Edition: The Lectures of 1827. Edited by Peter C. Hodgson. Berkeley: University of California Press, 1988.

Logic. Translated from the *Encyclopaedia of the Philosophical Sciences* by William Wallace. Oxford: Clarendon Press, 1982.

Natural Law. Translated by T. M. Knox. Philadelphia: University of Pennsylvania Press, 1975.

Phenomenology of Mind. Translated by J. B. Baillie. London: Allen and Unwin, 1931; reprint, New York: Harper and Row, 1967.

Phenomenology of Spirit. Translated by A. V. Miller with introduction and analysis by J. N. Findlay. Oxford: Clarendon Press, 1977.

Philosophical Propaedeutic. Translated by A. V. Miller. New York: Basil Blackwell, 1986.

Philosophy of Fine Art. 4 vols. Translated by F. P. B. Osmaston. London: G. Bell, 1920; reprint, New York: Hacker Art Books, 1975.

Philosophy of History. Translated by J. Sibree. New York: Colonial Press, 1899; reprint, New York: Dover, 1956.

Philosophy of Mind. Translated from the *Encyclopaedia of the Philosophical Sciences* by W. Wallace and A.V. Miller. Oxford: Clarendon Press, 1971.

Philosophy of Nature. 3 vols. Translated from the *Encyclopaedia of the Philosophical Sciences* by M. J. Petry. London: Allen and Unwin, 1970.

Philosophy of Nature. Translated from the *Encyclopaedia of the Philosophical Sciences* by A. V. Miller. Oxford: Clarendon Press, 1970.

Philosophy of Right. Translated by T. M. Knox. Oxford: Clarendon Press, 1952.

Philosophy of Subjective Spirit. 3 vols. Translated from the *Encyclopaedia of the Philosophical Sciences* by M. J. Petry. Dordrecht, Holland: D. Reidel. 1978.

Political Writings. Translated by T. M. Knox Oxford: Clarendon Press, 1965.

Reason in History. New York: Library of Liberal Arts, 1953. A translation by Robert S. Hartman of the *Introduction* to Hegel's *Lectures on the Philosophy of History*.

Science of Logic. Translated by A.V. Miller. London: Allen and Unwin, 1970.

Science of Logic. 2 vols. Translated by W. H. Johnston and L. G. Struthers. London: Allen and Unwin, 1929; reprint, Atlantic Highlands, NJ: Humanities Press, 1966.

System of Ethical Life and First Philosophy of Spirit. Translated by H. S. Harris and T. M. Knox. Albany: State University of New York Press, 1979.

Three Essays, 1793–1795: The Tübingen Essay, Berne Fragments, The Life of Jesus. Translated by Peter Fuss and John Dobbins. South Bend, IN: Notre Dame University Press, 1984.

Who Thinks Abstractly?. Translated by Walter Kaufmann in *Hegel: Reinterpretation, Texts, and Commentary*. New York: Doubleday, 1965.

II. Biographies

Caird, Edward, *Hegel*. Edinburgh: W. Blackwood & Sons, 1883; reprint, New York: AMS Press, 1972.

Mueller, Gustav Emil, *Hegel: The Man, His Vision and Work*. New York: Pagent Press, 1968.

Weidmann, Franz, *Hegel: An Illustrated Biography*. Translated by J. Neugroschel. New York: Pegasus, 1968.

III. General Studies

Findlay, John N., *Hegel: A Re-Examination*. New York: Macmillan, 1958; reprint, New York: Collier Books, 1962.

Inwood, Michael J. *Hegel*. London: Routledge & Kegan Paul, 1983.

Marcuse, Herbert, *Reason and Revolution: Hegel and the Rise of Social Theory*. Oxford: University Press, 1941; reprint, Atlantic Highlands, NJ: Humanities Press, 1983.

Mure, G.R.G., *An Introduction to Hegel*. Oxford: Clarendon Press, 1940.

Plant, Raymond, *Hegel*. London: Allen and Unwin; Bloomington: University of Indiana Press, 1973.

Rosen, Stanley, *G.W.F. Hegel*. New Haven: Yale University Press, 1974.

Singer, Peter, *Hegel*. Oxford: Clarendon Press, 1983.

Stace, Walter Terrance, *The Philosophy of Hegel: A Systematic Exposition* New York: Macmillan, 1924; reprint, New York: Dover Books, 1955.

Taylor, Charles, *Hegel*. Cambridge: Cambridge University Press, 1975.

IV. Studies of the "Phenomenology of Mind"

Flay, Joseph, *Hegel's Quest for Certainty*. Albany: State University of New York Press, 1984.

Hegel Society of America, *Method and Speculation in Hegel's "Phenomenology."* Proceedings of the Fifth Biennial Meeting, Pennsylvania State University, 1978. Atlantic Highlands, NJ: Humanities Press, 1982.

Heidegger, Martin, Hegel's *"Phenomenology of Spirit."*

Translated by Parvis Emad and Kenneth Maly. Bloomington: Indiana University Press. 1988.

Hyppolite, Jean, *Genesis and Structure of Hegel's "Phenomenology of Spirit."* Translated by Samuel Cherniak and John Heckman. Evanston, IL: Northwestern University Press, 1974.

Kaufmann, Walter, *Hegel: Reinterpretation, Texts, and Commentary.* New York: Doubleday, 1965.

Kainz, Howard P., *Hegel's Phenomenology, Part I: Analysis and Commentary.* Birmingham: University of Alabama, 1976.

——, *Hegel's Phenomenology, Part II: The Evolution of Ethical and Religious Consciousness to the Absolute Standpoint.* Athens: Ohio University Press, 1983.

Kojève, Alexandre, *Introduction to the Reading of Hegel: Lectures on the "Phenomenology of Spirit."* Translated by James H. Nichols, Jr. Ithaca, NY: Cornell University Press, 1980.

Lauer, Quentin, *A Reading of Hegel's "Phenomenology of Spirit."* New York: Fordham University Press, 1974.

Loewenberg, Jacob, *Hegel's "Phenomenology": Dialogues on the Life of Mind.* LaSalle, IL: Open Court, 1965.

Marx, Werner, *Hegel's "Phenomenology of Spirit": A Commentary on the Preface and Introduction.* Translated by Peter Heath. New York: Harper and Row, 1975.

Norman, Richard, *Hegel's "Phenomenology": A Philosophical Introduction.* Sussex, England: Sussex University Press, 1976.

Shklar, Judith M., *Freedom and Independence: A Study of the Political Ideas of Hegel's "Phenomenology of Mind."* Cambridge: Cambridge University Press, 1976.

Solomon, Robert, *In the Spirit of Hegel: A Study of G. W. F. Hegel's "Phenomenology of Spirit."* New York: Oxford University Press, 1983.

Verene, Donald Phillip, *Hegel's Recollection: A Study of Images in the "Phenomenology of Spirit".* Albany: State University of New York Press, 1985.

Westphal, Merold, *History and Truth in Hegel's "Phenomenology."* Atlantic Highlands, NJ: Humanities Press, 1977.

· · · · · · · ·

A number of learned societies devoted exclusively to the study of Hegel and Hegelianism have been formed in recent years. Among them is the Hegel Society of America, established in 1969. It has hosted many philosophical conferences, and publishes its own biannual journal, *The Owl of Minerva.* An English society was founded in 1979. It publishes *The Bulletin of the Hegel Society of Great Britain.* Two German societies exist, the *Hegel-Gesellschaft* and the *Hegel-Vereiningung.* Since 1958, the West German government has supported the research of the Hegel-Archiv at Bochum University, which is engaged in preparing a definitive edition of Hegel's works and publishes an annual journal, *Hegel-Studien.*

PREFACE TO THE PHENOMENOLOGY OF MIND

1. In the case of a philosophical work it seems not only superfluous, but, in view of the nature of philosophy, even inappropriate and misleading to begin, as writers usually do in a preface, by explaining the end the author had in mind, the circumstances which gave rise to the work, and the relation in which the writer takes it to stand to other treaties on the same subject, written by his predecessors or his contemporaries. For whatever it might be suitable to state about philosophy in a preface—say, an historical sketch of the main drift and point of view, the general content and results, a string of desultory

assertions and assurances about the truth—this cannot be accepted as the form and manner in which to expound philosophical truth.

2. Moreover, because philosophy has its being essentially in the element of that universality which encloses the particular within it, the end or final result seems, in the case of philosophy more than in that of other sciences,[1] to have absolutely expressed the complete fact itself in its very nature; contrasted with that the mere process of bringing it to light would seem, properly speaking, to have no essential significance. On the other hand, in the general idea of, e.g., anatomy—the knowledge of the parts of the body regarded as lifeless—we are quite sure we do not possess the objective concrete fact, the actual content of the science, but must, over and above, be concerned with particulars. Further, in the case of such a collection of items of knowledge, which has no real right to the name of science, any talk about purpose and suchlike generalities is not commonly very different from the descriptive and superficial way[2] in which the contents of the science—these nerves and muscles, etc.—are themselves spoken of. In philosophy, on the other hand, it would at once be felt incongruous were such a method made use of and yet shown by philosophy itself to be incapable of grasping the truth.

3. In the same way too, by determining the relation which a philosophical work professes to have to other treaties on the same subject, an extraneous interest is introduced, and

---

[1]Like others, Baillie has consistently translated the term *Wissenschaft* as "science." In German, however, and particularly in Hegel, *Wissenschaft* does not mean what the English "science" generally means today, namely, the controlled observation and exact mathematical measurement of physical objects or actions. Instead, *Wissenschaft* connotes systematic and assured knowledge of the fundamental principles governing any subject of study.

[2] . . . *historisch und begrifflos*, here translated as "descriptive and superficial," would have been better rendered as "historical and conceptually empty." See the note about *Begriff* on pp. 28–29.

obscurity is thrown over the point at issue in the knowledge of the truth. The more the ordinary mind takes the opposition between true and false to be fixed, the more is it accustomed to expect either agreement or contradiction with a given philosophical system, and only to see reason for the one or the other in any explanatory statement concerning such a system. It does not conceive the diversity of philosophical systems as the progressive evolution of truth; rather, it sees only contradiction in that variety. The bud disappears when the blossom breaks through, and we might say that the former is refuted by the latter; in the same way when the fruit comes, the blossom may be explained to be a false form of the plant's existence, for the fruit appears as its true nature in place of the blossom. These stages are not merely differentiated; they supplant one another as being incompatible with one another. But the ceaseless activity of their own inherent nature makes them at the same time moments of an organic unity, where they not merely do not contradict one another, but where one is as necessary as the other; and this equal necessity of all moments constitutes alone and thereby the life of the whole. But contradiction as between philosophical systems is not wont to be conceived in this way; on the other hand, the mind perceiving the contradiction does not commonly know how to relieve it or keep it free from its onesidedness, and to recognize in what seems conflicting and inherently antagonistic the presence of mutually necessary moments.

4. The demand for such explanations, as also the attempts to satisfy this demand, very easily pass for the essential business philosophy has to undertake. Where could the inmost truth of a philosophical work be found better expressed than in its purposes and results? And in what way could these be more definitely known than through their distinction from what is produced during the same period by others working in the same field? If, however, such procedure is to pass for more than the beginning of knowledge, if it is to pass for actually knowing, then we must, in point of fact, look on it as a device for avoiding the real business at issue, an attempt to combine the appearance of being in earnest and taking trouble about

the subject with an actual neglect of the subject altogether. For the real subject-matter is not exhausted in its purpose, but in working the matter out; nor is the mere result attained the concrete whole itself, but the result along with the process of arriving at it. The purpose by itself is a lifeless universal, just as the general drift is a mere activity in a certain direction, which is still without its concrete realization; and the naked result is the corpse of the system which has left its guiding tendency behind it. Similarly, the distinctive difference of anything is rather the boundary, the limit, of the subject; it is found at that point where the subject-matter stops, or it is what this subject-matter is *not*. To trouble oneself in this fashion with the purpose and results, and again with the differences, the positions taken up and judgments passed by one thinker and another, is therefore an easier task than perhaps it seems. For instead of laying hold of the matter in hand, a procedure of that kind is all the while away from the subject altogether. Instead of dwelling within it and becoming absorbed by it, knowledge of that sort is always grasping at something else; such knowledge, instead of keeping to the subject-matter and giving itself up to it, never gets away from itself. The easiest thing of all is to pass judgments on what has a solid substantial content; it is more difficult to grasp it, and most of all difficult to do both together and produce the systematic exposition of it.

5. The beginning of culture and of the struggle to pass out of the unbroken immediacy of naive psychical life has always to be made by acquiring knowledge of universal principles and points of view, by striving, in the first instance, to work up simply to the *thought* of the subject-matter in general, not forgetting at the same time to give reasons for supporting it or refuting it, to apprehend the concrete riches and fullness contained in its various determinate qualities, and to know how to furnish a coherent, orderly account of it and a responsible judgment upon it. This beginning of mental cultivation will, however, very soon make way for the earnestness of actual life in all its fullness, which leads to a living experience of the subject-matter itself; and when, in addition, conceptual

thought strenuously penetrates to the very depths of its meaning, such knowledge and style of judgment will keep their due place in everyday thought and conversation.

6. The systematic development of truth in scientific form can alone be the true shape in which truth exists. To help to bring philosophy nearer to the form of science—that goal where it can lay aside the name of *love* of knowledge and be actual *knowledge*—that is what I have set before me. The inner necessity that knowledge should be science lies in its very nature; and the adequate and sufficient explanation for this lies simply and solely in the systematic exposition of philosophy itself. The external necessity, however, so far as this is apprehended in a universal way, and apart from the accident of the personal element and the particular occasioning influences affecting the individual, is the same as the internal: it lies in the form and shape in which the process of time presents the existence of its moments. To show that the time process does raise philosophy to the level of scientific system would, therefore, be the only true justification of the attempts which aim at proving that philosophy must assume this character; because the temporal process would thus bring out and lay bare the necessity of it, nay, more, would at the same time be carrying out that very aim itself.

7. When we state the true form of truth to be its scientific character—or, what is the same thing, when it is maintained that truth finds the medium of its existence in notions or conceptions alone—I know that this seems to contradict an idea with all its consequences which makes great pretensions and has gained widespread acceptance and conviction at the present time. A word of explanation concerning this contradiction seems, therefore, not out of place, even though at this stage it can amount to no more than a dogmatic assurance exactly like the view we are opposing. If, that is to say, truth exists merely in what, or rather exists merely *as* what, is called at one time intuition, at another immediate knowledge of the Absolute, Religion, Being—not being in the center of divine love, but the very Being of this center, of the Absolute itself—

from that point of view it is rather the opposite of the notional or conceptual form which would be required for systematic philosophical exposition. The Absolute on this view is not to be grasped in conceptual form, but felt, intuited; it is not its conception, but the feeling of it and intuition of it that are to have the say and find expression.[3]

8. If we consider the appearance of a claim like this in its more general setting, and look at the level which the self-conscious mind at present occupies, we shall find that self-consciousness has got beyond the substantial fullness of life, which it used to carry on in the element of thought—beyond the state of immediacy of belief, beyond the satisfaction and security arising from the assurance which consciousness possessed of being reconciled with ultimate reality and with its all-pervading presence, within as well as without. Self-conscious mind has not merely passed beyond that to the opposite extreme of insubstantial reflection of self into self, but beyond this too. It has not merely lost its essential and concrete life, it is also conscious of this loss and of the transitory finitude characteristic of its content. Turning away from the husks it has to feed on, and confessing that it lies in wickedness and sin, it reviles itself for so doing, and now desires from philosophy not so much to bring it to a knowledge of what it is, as to obtain once again through philosophy the restoration of that sense of solidity and substantiality of existence it has lost.[4] Philosophy is thus expected not so much to meet this want by opening up the compact solidity of substantial existence, and bringing this to the light and level of self-con-

---

[3]A reference to the views of such early romantics as Friedrich H. Jacobi (1743–1819), Friedrich von Schlegel (1772–1829), and Daniel F. Schleiermacher (1768–1834). These and other romantics disparaged the intellect and taught that immediate feeling and sensibility are the best means of apprehending truth. They believed that faith and feeling, not reason, are the proper tools of philosophy.

[4]An apparent allusion to the parable of the prodigal son; see Luke, 15: 16ff.

sciousness—is not so much to bring chaotic conscious life back to the orderly ways of thought, and the simplicity of the notion, as to run together what thought has divided asunder, suppress the notion with its distinctions, and restore the *feeling* of existence. What it wants from philosophy is not so much insight as edification. The beautiful, the holy, the eternal, religion, love—these are the bait required to awaken the desire to bite: not the notion, but ecstasy, not the march of cold necessity in the subject-matter, but ferment and enthusiasm—these are to be the ways by which the wealth of the concrete substance is to be stored and increasingly extended.

9. With this demand there goes the strenuous effort, almost perfervidly zealous in its activity, to rescue mankind from being sunken in what is sensuous, vulgar, and of fleeting importance, and to raise men's eyes to the stars; as if men had quite forgotten the divine, and were on the verge of finding satisfaction, like worms, in mud and water. Time was when man had a heaven, decked and fitted out with endless wealth of thoughts and pictures. The significance of all that is, lay in the thread of light by which it was attached to heaven; instead of dwelling in the present as it is here and now, the eye glanced away over the present to the Divine, away, so to say, to a present that lies beyond. The mind's gaze had to be directed under compulsion to what is earthly, and kept fixed there; and it has needed a long time to introduce that clearness, which only celestial realities had, into the crassness and confusion shrouding the sense of things earthly, and to make attention to the immediate present as such, which was called Experience, of interest and of value.[5] Now we have apparently the need for the opposite of all this; man's mind and interest are so deeply rooted in the earthly that we require a like power to have them raised above that level. His spirit shows such poverty of nature

[5]Perhaps referring to the English philosopher Francis Bacon (1561–1626). Hegel treated him extensively and favorably in his *Lectures on the History of Philosophy*, and joined those who esteemed Bacon "as the man who directed knowledge to its true source, to experience . . ."

that it seems to long for the mere pitiful feeling of the divine in the abstract, and to get refreshment from that, like a wanderer in the desert craving for the merest mouthful of water. By the little which can thus satisfy the needs of the human spirit we can measure the extent of its loss.

10. This easy contentment in receiving, or stinginess in giving, does not suit the character of science. The man who only seeks edification, who wants to envelop in mist the manifold diversity of his earthly existence and thought, and craves after the vague enjoyment of this vague and indeterminate Divinity—he may look where he likes to find this: he will easily find for himself the means to procure something he can rave over and puff himself up withal. But philosophy must beware of wishing to be edifying.[6]

11. Still less must this kind of contentment, which holds science in contempt, take upon itself to claim that raving obscurantism of this sort is something higher than science. These apocalyptic utterances pretend to occupy the very center and the deepest depths; they look askance at all definiteness and preciseness ($\acute{o}\rho o\varsigma$) of meaning; and they deliberately hold back from conceptual thinking and the constraining necessities of thought, as being the sort of reflecton which, they say, can only feel at home in the sphere of finitude. But just as there is a breadth which is emptiness, there is a depth which is empty too: as we may have an extension of substance which overflows into finite multiplicity without the power of keeping the manifold together, in the same way we may have an insubstantial intensity which, keeping itself in as mere force without actual expression, is no better than superficiality. The

[6]The Danish existentialist Søren Kierkegaard (1813–1855) might have had this remark in mind when he wrote his series of *Edifying Discourses* (1843–1844). In any case, as Kierkegaard wrote, "It is strange what hate, conspicuous everywhere, Hegel has for the up-building or the edifying . . ." *Journals and Papers*, ed. and trans. by Howard V. Hong and Edna H. Hong (Bloomington: Indiana University Press, 1970), 2, p. 214. See below, n. 19.

force of mind is only as great as its expression; its depth only as deep as its power to expand and lose itself when spending and giving out its substance. Moreover, when this unreflective emotional knowledge makes a pretense of having immersed its own very self in the depths of the absolute Being, and of philosophizing in all holiness and truth, it hides from itself the fact that instead of devotion to God, it rather, by this contempt for all measurable precision and definiteness, simply attests in its own case the fortuitous character of its content, and in the other endows God with its own caprice. When such minds commit themselves to the unrestrained ferment of sheer emotion, they think that, by putting a veil over self-consciousness, and surrendering all understanding, they are thus God's beloved ones to whom He gives His wisdom in sleep.[7] This is the reason, too, that in point of fact what they do conceive and bring forth in sleep is dreams.

12. For the rest it is not difficult to see that our epoch is a birth-time, and a period of transition. The spirit of man has broken with the old order of things hitherto prevailing, and with the old ways of thinking, and is in the mind to let them all sink into the depths of the past and to set about its own transformation. It is indeed never at rest, but carried along the stream of progress ever onward. But it is here as in the case of the birth of a child; after a long period of nutrition in silence, the continuity of the gradual growth in size, of quantitative change, is suddenly cut short by the first breath drawn—there is a break in the process, a qualitative change—and the child is born.[8] In like manner the spirit of the time, growing slowly

---

[7]See Psalm 127:2.

[8]This process of development has long been used by Marxists as a justification for revolutionary change. Thus Joseph Stalin wrote, "If the passing of slow quantitative changes into rapid and abrupt qualitative changes is a law of development, then it is clear that revolutions made by oppressed classes are a quite natural and inevitable phenomenon." *Dialectical and Historical Materialism* (New York: International Publishers, 1940), p. 8.

and quietly ripe for the new form it is to assume, disintegrates one fragment after another of the structure of its previous world. That it is tottering to its fall is indicated only by symptoms here and there. Frivolity and again ennui, which are spreading in the established order of things, the undefined foreboding of something unknown—all these betoken that there is something else approaching.[9] This gradual crumbling to pieces, which did not alter the general look and aspect of the whole, is interrupted by the sunrise, which, in a flash and at a single stroke, brings to view the form and structure of the new world.

13. But this new world is perfectly realized just as little as the new-born child; and it is essential to bear this in mind. It comes on the stage to begin with in its immediacy, in its bare generality. A building is not finished when its foundation is laid; and just as little is the attainment of a general notion of a whole the whole itself. When we want to see an oak with all its vigor of trunk, its spreading branches, and mass of foliage, we are not satisfied to be shown an acorn instead. In the same way science, the crowning glory of a spiritual world, is not found complete in its initial stages. The beginning of the new spirit is the outcome of a widespread revolution in manifold forms of spiritual culture; it is the reward which comes after a checkered and devious course of development, and after much struggle and effort. It is a whole which, after running its course and laying bare all its content, returns again to itself; it is the resultant abstract notion of the whole. But the actual realization of this abstract whole is only found when those previous shapes and forms, which are now reduced to ideal moments of the whole, are developed anew again, but developed and shaped within this new medium, and with the meaning they have thereby acquired.

14. While the new world makes its first appearance merely in general outline, merely as a whole lying concealed and

---

[9]Hegel is evidently alluding to what he saw as the character of French aristocracy just prior to the revolution of 1789.

hidden within a bare abstraction, the wealth of the bygone life, on the other hand, is still consciously present in recollection. Consciousness misses in the new form the detailed expanse of content; but still more the developed expression of form by which distinctions are definitely determined and arranged in their precise relations. Without this last feature science has no general intelligibility, and has the appearance of being an esoteric possession of a few individuals—an esoteric possession, because in the first instance it is only the essential principle or notion of science, only its inner nature that is to be found; and a possession of few individuals, because, at its first appearance, its content is not elaborated and expanded in detail, and thus its existence is turned into something particular. Only what is perfectly determinate in form is at the same time exoteric, comprehensible, and capable of being learned and possessed by everybody. Intelligibility is the form in which science is offered to everyone, and is the open road to it made plain for all. To reach rational knowledge by our intelligence is the just demand of the mind which comes to science. For intelligence, understanding (*Verstand*), is thinking, pure activity of the self in general; and what is intelligible (*Verständige*) is something from the first familiar and common to the scientific and unscientific mind alike, enabling the unscientific mind to enter the domain of science.

15. Science, at its commencement, when as yet it has reached neither detailed completeness nor perfection of form, is exposed to blame on that account. But it would be as unjust to suppose this blame to attach to its essential nature, as it is inadmissible not to be ready to recognize the demand for that further development in fuller detail. In the contrast and opposition between these two aspects (the initial and the developed stages of science) seems to lie the critical knot which scientific culture at present struggles to loosen, and about which so far it is not very clear. One side parades the wealth of its material and the intelligibility of its ideas; the other pours contempt at any rate on the latter, and makes a parade of the immediate intuitive rationality and divine quality of its con-

tent. Although the first is reduced to silence, perhaps by the inner force of truth alone, perhaps, too, by the noisy bluster of the other side, and even though having regard to the reason and nature of the case it did feel overborne, yet it does not therefore feel satisfied as regards those demands for greater development; for those demands are just, but still unfulfilled. Its silence is due only in part to the victory of the other side; it is half due to that weariness and indifference which are usually the consequence when expectations are being constantly awakened by promises which are not followed up by performance.

16. The other side[10] no doubt at times makes an easy enough matter of having a vast expanse of content. They haul on to their territory a lot of material, that, namely, which is already familiar and arranged in order; and since they are concerned more especially about what is exceptional, strange, and curious, they seem all the more to be in possession of the rest, which knowledge in its own way was finished and done with, as well as to have control over what was unregulated and disorderly. Hence everything appears brought within the compass of the Absolute Idea, which seems thus to be recognized in everything, and to have succeeded in becoming a system *in extenso* of scientific knowledge. But if we look more closely at this expanded system we find that it has not been reached by one and the same principle taking shape in diverse ways; it is

[10]"The other side": here evidently the disciples of Hegel's former colleague, F. W. Schelling. This school of thought envisioned all particular things and ideas as contained under one all-encompassing idea—the Absolute. But to Hegel, such an attempt to simply ignore the reality of differences would create nothing but general confusion. On the other hand, the French Enlightenment produced such schools as the Encyclopedists. These thinkers, such as Denis Diderot (1713–1784), diligently sought to gather together all bits of knowledge so as to create a grand sum of all knowledge—a massive and all-encompassing encyclopedia. Both schools had antithetical methods: Schelling's school began with an Absolute that generated all particulars, and the Encyclopedists generated an Absolute out of the totality of particulars.

the shapeless repetition of one and the same idea, which is applied in an external fashion to different material, the wearisome reiteration of it keeping up the semblance of diversity. The Idea, which by itself is no doubt the truth, really never gets any farther than just where it began, as long as the development of it consists in nothing else than such a repetition of the same formula. If the knowing subject carries around everywhere the one inert abstract form, taking up in external fashion whatever material comes his way, and dipping it into this element, then this comes about as near to fulfilling what is wanted—viz. a self-origination of the wealth of detail, and a self-determining distinction of shapes and forms—as any chance fancies about the content in question. It is rather a monochrome formalism, which only arrives at distinction in the matter it has to deal with, because this is already prepared and well known.

17. This monotonousness and abstract universality are maintained to be the Absolute. This formalism insists that to be dissatisfied therewith argues an incapacity to grasp the standpoint of the Absolute, and keep a firm hold on it. If it was once the case that the bare possibility of thinking of something in some other fashion was sufficient to refute a given idea, and the naked possibility, the bare general thought, possessed and passed for the entire substantive value of actual knowledge; similarly we find here all the value ascribed to the general idea in this bare form without concrete realization; and we see here, too, the style and method of speculative contemplation identified with dissipating and resolving what is determinate and distinct, or rather with hurling it down, without more ado and without any justification, into the abyss of vacuity. To consider any specific fact as it is in the Absolute, consists here in nothing else than saying about it that, while it is now doubtless spoken of as something specific, yet in the Absolute, in the abstract identity $A = A$, there is no such thing at all, for everything is there all one. To pit this single assertion, that "in the Absolute all is one," against the organized whole of determinate and complete knowledge, or of knowledge which at

least aims at and demands complete development—to give out its Absolute as the night in which, as we say, all cows are black[11]—that is the very *naïveté* of emptiness of knowledge.

18. The formalism which has been deprecated and despised by recent philosophy, and which has arisen once more in philosophy itself, will not disappear from science, even though its inadequacy is known and felt, till the knowledge of absolute reality has become quite clear as to what its own true nature consists in. Having in mind that the general idea of what is to be done, if it precedes the attempt to carry it out, facilitates the comprehension of this process, it is worthwhile to indicate here some rough idea of it, with the hope at the same time that this will give us the opportunity to set aside certain forms whose habitual presence is a hindrance in the way of speculative knowledge.

19. In my view—a view which the developed exposition of the system itself can alone justify—everything depends on grasping and expressing the ultimate truth not as Substance but as Subject as well. At the same time we must note that concrete substantiality implicates and involves the universal or the immediacy of knowledge itself, as well as that immediacy which is being, or immediacy *qua* object *for* knowledge. If the generation which heard God spoken of as the One Substance[12] was shocked and revolted by such a characteriza-

---

[11]"oder sein Absolutes für die Nacht auszugeben, worin, wie man zu sagen pflegt, alle Kühe schwarz sind." Wolfgang Mieder, in his *Encyclopedia of World Proverbs* (Englewood Cliffs, NJ: Prentice-Hall, 1986) identifies this as a Yiddish proverb. Another version of it (one of many) is the Slovakian "After dark every cow is black." Goethe, with whom Hegel was personally acquainted, expressed a similar thought in *Faust*, Part II, Act I: "Who can tell friend from villain in the night,/ When all the cows are black, all catseyes bright?" *Faust*, ed. Cyrus Hamlin, trans. Walter Arndt (New York: W. W. Norton, 1976), p. 128.

[12]A reference to Benedict Spinoza (1632–1677), whose work *Ethics* maintains that all things are but attributes or modes of one infinite substance, an "Absolute Substance," which he calls "God."

tion of his nature, the reason lay partly in the instinctive feeling that in such a conception self-consciousness was simply submerged, and not preserved. But partly, again, the opposite position, which maintains thinking to be merely subjective thinking, abstract universality as such, is exactly the same bare uniformity, is undifferentiated, unmoved substantiality.[13] And even if, in the third place, thought combines with itself the being of substance, and conceives immediacy or intuition (*Anschauung*) as thinking, it is still a question whether this intellectual intuition does not fall back into that inert, abstract simplicity, and exhibit and expound reality itself in an unreal manner.[14]

20. The living substance, further, is that being which is truly subject, or, what is the same thing, is truly realized and actual (*wirklich*) solely in the process of positing itself, or in mediating with its own self its transitions from one state or position to the opposite. As subject it is pure and simple negativity, and just on that account a process of splitting up what is simple and undifferentiated, a process of duplicating and setting factors in opposition, which [process] in turn is the negation of this indifferent diversity and of the opposition of factors it entails. True reality is merely this process of reinstating self-identity, of reflecting into its own self in and from its other, and is not an original and primal unity as such, not an immediate unity as such. It is the process of its own becoming, the circle which presupposes its end as its purpose, and has its end for its beginning; it becomes concrete and actual only by being carried out, and by the end it involves.

21. The life of God and divine intelligence, then, can, if we like, be spoken of as love disporting with itself; but this idea

[13]Here Hegel is referring to Immanuel Kant (1724–1804), who in his *Critique of Pure Reason* maintained that our experience and our understanding were predetermined and conditioned by innate (a priori) structures of thought, and not by the actual nature of things in themselves (*ding-an-sich*).

[14]A reference to F. W. Schelling; see above, n. 10.

falls into edification, and even sinks into insipidity, if it lacks the seriousness, the suffering, the patience, and the labor of the negative. *Per se*[15] the divine life is no doubt undisturbed identity and oneness with itself, which finds no serious obstacle in otherness and estrangement, and none in the surmounting of this estrangement. But this "per se" is abstract generality, where we abstract from its real nature, which consists in its being objective to itself, conscious of itself on its own account (*für sich zu sein*); and where consequently we neglect altogether the self-movement which is the formal character of its activity. If the form is declared to correspond to the essence, it is just for that reason a misunderstanding to suppose that knowledge can be content with the "per se," the essence, but can do without the form, that the absolute principle, or absolute intuition, makes the carrying out of the former, or the development of the latter, needless. Precisely because the form is as necessary to the essence as the essence to itself, absolute reality must not be conceived of and expressed as essence alone, i.e., as immediate substance, or as pure self-intuition of the Divine, but as form also, and with the entire wealth of the developed form. Only then is it grasped and expressed as really actual.

22. The truth is the whole. The whole, however, is merely the essential nature reaching its completeness through the process of its own development. Of the Absolute it must be said that it is essentially a result, that only at the end is it what

---

[15]See above, n. 13. *An Sich* is here translated as *per se*, but insofar as this particular passage follows an allusion to Kant, perhaps "in itself" would be better. "In itself," or *an sich*, generally means that something is understood in an absolute sense, without reference to another or even to itself. It is a mere "thing" existing without either external or internal relationships. On the other hand, "for itself," or *für sich*, means a relational object, either a "being for" other things or a self-relating (self-conscious) being. Jean-Paul Sartre's famous distinction between the *en soi* ("in itself") and the *pour soi* ("for itself") derives from Hegel's distinction.

it is in very truth; and just in that consists its nature, which is to be actual, subject, or self-becoming, self-development. Should it appear contradictory to say that the Absolute has to be conceived essentially as a result, a little consideration will set this appearance of contradiction in its true light. The beginning, the principle, or the Absolute, as at first or immediately expressed, is merely the universal. If we say "all animals," that does not pass for zoology; for the same reason we see at once that the words absolute, divine, eternal, and so on do not express what is implied in them; and only mere words like these, in point of fact, express intuition as the immediate. Whatever is more than a word like that, even the mere transition to a proposition, is a form of mediation, contains a process towards another state from which we must return once more. It is this process of mediation, however, that is rejected with horror, as if absolute knowledge were being surrendered when more is made of mediation than merely the assertion that it is nothing absolute, and does not exist in the Absolute.

23. This horrified rejection of mediation, however, arises as a fact from want of acquaintance with its nature, and with the nature of absolute knowledge itself. For mediating is nothing but self-identity working itself out through an active self-directed process; or, in other words, it is reflection into self, the aspect in which the ego is for itself, objective to itself. It is pure negativity, or, reduced to its utmost abstraction, the process of bare and simple becoming. The ego, or becoming in general, this process of mediating, is, because of its being simple, just immediacy coming to be, and is immediacy itself. We misconceive therefore the nature of reason if we exclude reflection or mediation from ultimate truth, and do not take it to be a positive moment of the Absolute. It is reflection which constitutes truth the final result, and yet at the same time does away[16] with the contrast between result and the process of

---

[16] . . . *aber diesen Gegensatz gegen sein Werden ebenso aufhebt* . . . The term "aufhebt" is here translated as "does away with." For a fuller understanding of the significance of the term *Aufhebung* (whence *aufhebt*) in Hegel's philosophy, see "Translator's Notes," p. 28.

arriving at it. For this process is likewise simple, and therefore not distinct from the form of truth, which consists in appearing as simple in the result; it is indeed just this restoration and return to simplicity. While the embryo is certainly, in itself, implicitly a human being, it is not so explicitly, it is not by itself a human being;[17] man is explicitly man only in the form of developed and cultivated reason, which has made itself to be what it is implicitly. Its actual reality is first found here. But this result arrived at is itself simple immediacy; for it is self-conscious freedom, which is at one with itself, and has not set aside the opposition it involves and left it there, but has made its account with it and become reconciled to it.

24. What has been said may also be expressed by saying that reason is purposive activity. The exaltation of so-called nature at the expense of thought misconceived, and more especially the rejection of external purposiveness, have brought the idea of purpose in general into disrepute. All the same, in the sense in which Aristotle, too, characterizes nature as purposive activity, purpose is the immediate, the undisturbed, the unmoved which is self-moving;[18] as such it is subject. Its power of moving, taken abstractly, is its existence for itself, or pure negativity. The result is the same as the beginning solely because the beginning is purpose. Stated otherwise, what is actual and concrete is the same as its inner principle or notion simply because the immediate *qua* purpose contains within it the self or pure actuality. The realized purpose, or concrete actuality, is movement and development unfolded. But this very unrest is the self; and it is one and the same with that immediacy and simplicity characteristic of the beginning just for the reason that it is the result, and has

[17] *Wenn der Embryo wohl* an sich *Mensch ist er es aber nicht* für sich. See above, n. 15.

[18] Hegel admired Aristotle (385–322 B.C.) and knew his works well. He is referring here to Aristotle's *Metaphysics* (bk. 12) and *Physics* (bks. 7 and 8). Here God is described as "self-thinking thought," and as the "unmoved mover" who moves all things by being their "end," the "Highest Good" which they strive to emulate.

returned upon itself—while this latter again is just the self, and the self is self-referring and self-relating identity and simplicity.[19]

25. The need to think of the Absolute as subject, has led men to make use of statements like "God is the eternal," the "moral order of the world," or "love," etc. In such propositions the truth is just barely stated to be Subject, but not set forth as the process of reflectively mediating itself with itself. In a proposition of that kind we begin with the word God. By itself this is a meaningless sound, a mere name; the predicate says afterwards *what* it is, gives it content and meaning: the empty beginning becomes real knowledge only when we thus get to the end of the statement. So far as that goes, why not speak alone of the eternal, of the moral order of the world, etc., or, like the ancients, of pure conceptions such as being, the one, etc., i.e., of what gives the meaning without adding the meaningless sound at all?[20] But this word just indicates that it is not a being or essence or universal in general that is put forward, but something reflected into self, a subject. Yet at the same time this acceptance of the Absolute as Subject is merely anticipated, not really affirmed. The subject is taken to be a fixed point, and to it as their support the predicates are attached, by a process falling within the individual knowing about it, but not looked upon as belonging to the point of attachment itself; only by such a process, however, could the content be presented as subject. Constituted as it is, this process cannot belong to the subject; but when that point of support is fixed to start with, this process cannot be otherwise constituted, it can only be external. The anticipation that the

---

[19]This difficult passage is echoed (partly in parody) in Kierkegaard's *Sickness Unto Death* (1844), pt. 1, sec. a. The precise extent to which Kierkegaard was indebted to Hegel is a controversial matter, but certainly a knowledge of Hegel is invaluable for fully understanding a great deal of Kierkegaard's writings.

[20]Referring to the Eleatic school, established by Parmenides about 500 B.C. See below, n. 38.

Absolute is subject is therefore not merely not the realization of this conception; it even makes realization impossible. For it makes out the notion to be a static point, while its actual reality is self-movement, self-activity.

26. Among the many consequences that follow from what has been said, it is of importance to emphasize this, that knowledge is only real and can only be set forth fully in the form of science, in the form of system; and further, that a so-called fundamental proposition or first principle of philosophy, even if it is true, is yet none the less false just because and in so far as it is merely a fundamental proposition, merely a first principle. It is for that reason easily refuted. The refutation consists in bringing out its defective character; and it *is* defective because it is merely the universal, merely a principle, the beginning. If the refutation is complete and thorough, it is derived and developed from the nature of the principle itself, and not accomplished by bringing in from elsewhere other counter assurances and chance fancies. It would be strictly the development of the principle, and thus the completion of its deficiency, were it not that it misunderstands its own purport by taking account solely of the negative aspect of what it seeks to do, and is not conscious of the positive character of its process and result. The really positive working out of the beginning is at the same time just as much the very reverse, it is a negative attitude towards the principle we start from, negative, that is to say, of its one-sided form, which consists in being primarily immediate, a mere purpose. It may therefore be regarded as a refutation of what constitutes the basis of the system; but more correctly it should be looked at as a demonstration that the *basis* or principle of the system is in point of fact merely its *beginning*.

27. That the truth is only realized in the form of system, that substance is essentially subject, is expressed in the idea which represents the Absolute as Spirit (*Geist*)—the grandest conception of all, and one which is due to modern times and its religion. Spirit is alone Reality. It is the inner being of the world, that which essentially is, and is *per se*; it assumes

objective, determinate form, and enters into relations with itself—it is externality (otherness), and exists for self; yet, in this determination, and in its otherness, it is still one with itself—it is self-contained and self-complete, in itself and for itself at once. This self-containedness, however, is first something known by us, it is implicit in its nature (*an sich*); it is Substance spiritual. It has to become self-contained *for itself*, on its own account; it must be knowledge of spirit, and must be consciousness of itself as spirit. This means, it must be presented to itself as an object, but at the same time straightway annul and transcend this objective form; it must be its own object in which it finds itself reflected. So far as its spiritual content is produced by its own activity, it is only *we* [the thinkers] who know spirit to be for itself, to be objective to itself; but in so far as spirit knows itself to be for itself, then this self-production, the pure notion, is the sphere and element in which its objectification takes effect, and where it gets its existential form. In this way it is in its existence aware of itself as an object in which its own self is reflected. Mind, which, when thus developed, knows itself to be mind, is science. Science is its realization, and the kingdom it sets up for itself in its own native element.

28. A self having knowledge purely of itself in the absolute antithesis of itself, this pure ether as such, is the very soil where science flourishes, is knowledge in universal form. The beginning of philosophy presupposes or demands from consciousness that it should feel at home in this element. But this element only attains its perfect meaning and acquires transparency through the process of gradually developing it. It is pure spirituality as the universal which assumes the shape of simple immediacy; and this simple element, existing as such, is the field of science, is thinking, which can be only in mind. Because this medium, this immediacy of mind, is the mind's substantial nature in general, it is the transfigured essence, reflection which itself is simple, which is aware of itself as immediacy; it is being, which is reflection into itself. Science on its side requires the individual self-consciousness to have

risen into this high ether, in order to be able to live with science, and in science, and really to feel alive there. Conversely the individual has the right to demand that science shall hold the ladder to help him to get at least as far as this position, shall show him that he has in himself this ground to stand on. His right rests on his absolute independence, which he knows he possesses in every type and phase of knowledge; for in every phase, whether recognized by science or not, and whatever be the content, his right as an individual is the absolute and final form, i.e., he is the immediate certainty of self, and thereby is unconditioned being, were this expression preferred. If the position taken up by consciousness, that of knowing about objective things as opposed to itself, and about itself as opposed to them, is held by science to be the very opposite of what science is: if, when in knowing it keeps within itself and never goes beyond itself, science holds this state to be rather the loss of mind altogether—on the other hand the element in which *science* consists is looked at by consciousness as a remote and distant region, in which consciousness is no longer in possession of itself. Each of these two sides takes the other to be the perversion of the truth. For the naïve consciousness, to give itself up completely and straight away to science is to make an attempt, induced by some unknown influence, all at once to walk on its head. The compulsion to take up this attitude and move about in this position, is a constraining force it is urged to fall in with, without ever being prepared for it and with no apparent necessity for doing so. Let science be *per se* what it likes, in its relation to naïve immediate self-conscious life it presents the appearance of being a reversal of the latter; or, again, because naïve self-consciousness finds the principle of its reality in the certainty of itself, science bears the character of unreality, since consciousness "for itself" is a state quite outside of science. Science has for that reason to combine that other element of self-certainty with its own, or rather to show that the other element belongs to itself, and how it does so. When devoid of that sort of reality, science is merely the content of mind *qua* something implicit or potential (*an sich*); purpose, which at the start is no more than something internal; not spirit, but at first merely spiritual substance. This implicit moment (*Ansich*) has to find external expression, and become objective on its own account. This means nothing else than that this moment has to establish self-consciousness as one with itself.

29. It is this process by which science in general comes about, this gradual development of knowing, that is set forth here in the *Phenomenology of Mind*.[21] Knowing, as it is found at the start, mind in its immediate and primitive stage, is without the essential nature of mind, is sense-consciousness. To reach the stage of genuine knowledge, or produce the element where science is found—the pure conception of science itself—a long and laborious journey must be undertaken. This process towards science, as regards the content it will bring to light and the forms it will assume in the course of its progress, will not be what is primarily imagined by leading the unscientific consciousness up to the level of science: it will be something different, too, from establishing and laying the foundations of science; and anyway something else than the sort of ecstatic enthusiasm which starts straight off with absolute knowledge, as if shot out of a pistol, and makes short work of other points of view simply by explaining that it is to take no notice of them.

30. The task of conducting the individual mind from its unscientific standpoint to that of science had to be taken in its general sense; we had to contemplate the formative development (*Bildung*) of the universal [or general] individual, of self-conscious spirit. As to the relation between these two [the particular and general individual], every moment, as it gains concrete form and its owner proper shape and appearance,

[21]The title of the first edition of Hegel's *Phenomenology* was: *System of Science: First Part: The Phenomenology of Mind*. In later editions Hegel reduced this to *The Phenomenology of Mind*.

finds a place in the life of the universal individual. The particular individual is incomplete mind, a concrete shape in whose existence, taken as a whole, one determinate characteristic predominates, while the others are found only in blurred outline. In that mind which stands higher than another the lower concrete form of existence has sunk into an obscure moment; what was formerly an objective fact (*die Sache selbst*) is now only a single trace: its definite shape has been veiled, and become simply a piece of shading. The individual, whose substance is mind at the higher level, passes through these past forms, much in the way that one who takes up a higher science goes through those preparatory forms of knowledge, which he has long made his own, in order to call up their content before him; he brings back the recollection of them without stopping to fix his interest upon them. The particular individual, so far as content is concerned, has also to go through the stages through which the general mind has passed, but as shapes once assumed by mind and now laid aside, as stages of a road which has been worked over and levelled out. Hence it is that, in the case of various kinds of knowledge, we find that what in former days occupied the energies of men of mature mental ability sinks to the level of information, exercises, and even pastimes, for children; and in this educational progress we can see the history of the world's culture delineated in faint outline. This bygone mode of existence has already become an acquired possession of the general mind, which constitutes the substance of the individual, and, by thus appearing externally to him, furnishes his inorganic nature. In this respect culture or development of mind (*Bildung*), regarded from the side of the individual, consists in his acquiring what lies at his hand ready for him, in making its inorganic nature organic to himself, and taking possession of it for himself. Looked at, however, from the side of universal mind *qua* general spiritual substance, culture means nothing else than that this substance gives itself its own self-consciousness, brings about its own inherent process and its own reflection into self.

31. Science lays before us the morphogenetic process of this cultural development in all its detailed fullness and necessity, and at the same time shows it to be something that has already sunk into the mind as a moment of its being and become a possession of mind. The goal to be reached is the mind's insight into what knowing is. Impatience asks for the impossible, wants to reach the goal without the means of getting there. The length of the journey has to be borne with, for every moment is necessary; and again we must halt at every stage, for each is itself a complete individual form, and is fully and finally considered only so far as its determinate character is taken and dealt with as a rounded and concrete whole, or only so far as the whole is looked at in the light of the special and peculiar character which this determination gives it. Because the substance of individual mind, nay, more, because the universal mind at work in the world (*Weltgeist*), has had the patience to go through these forms in the long stretch of time's extent, and to take upon itself the prodigious labor of the world's history, where it bodied forth in each form the entire content of itself, as each is capable of presenting it; and because by nothing less could that all-pervading mind ever manage to become conscious of what itself is—for that reason, the individual mind, in the nature of the case, cannot expect by less toil to grasp what its own substance contains. All the same, its task has meanwhile been made much lighter, because this has historically been implicitly (*an sich*) accomplished, the content is one where reality is already cancelled for spiritual possibilities, where immediacy has been overcome and brought under the control of reflection, the various forms and shapes have been already reduced to their intellectual abbreviations, to determinations of thought (*Gedankenbestimmung*) pure and simple. Being now a thought, the content is the property of the substance of mind; existence has no more to be changed into the form of what is inherent and implicit (*Ansichseins*), but only the implicit—no longer merely something primitive, nor lying hidden within existence, but already present as a recollection—into the form of what is explicit, of what is objective to self (*Fürsichseins*).

32. We have to state more exactly the way this is done. At the point at which we here take up this movement, we are spared, in connection with the whole, the process of cancelling and transcending the stage of mere existence. This process has already taken place. What is still to be done and needs a higher kind of transformation, is to transcend the forms as ideally presented and made familiar to our minds.[22] By that previous negative process, existence, having been withdrawn into the mind's substance, is, in the first instance, transferred to the life of self only in an immediate way. The property the self has thereby acquired, has still the same character of uncomprehended immediacy, of passive indifference, which existence itself had; existence has in this way merely passed into the form of an ideal presentation. At the same time, by so doing, it is something familiar to us, something "well-known," something which the existent mind has finished and done with, and hence takes no more to do with and no further interest in. While the activity that is done with the existent is itself merely the process of the particular mind, of mind which is not comprehending itself, on the other hand, *knowledge* is directed against this ideal presentation which has hereby arisen, against this "being-familiar" and "well-known"; it is an action of *universal* mind, the concern of *thought*.

33. What is "familiarly known" is not properly known, just for the reason that it is "familiar." When engaged in the process of knowing, it is the commonest form of self-deception, and a deception of other people as well, to assume something to be familiar, and give assent to it on that very account. Knowledge of that sort, with all its talk, never gets from the spot, but has no idea that this is the case. Subject and object, and so on, God, nature, understanding, sensibility, etc., are uncritically presupposed as familiar and something valid, and become fixed points from which to start and to which to return. The process of knowing flits between these secure points, and in consequence goes on merely along the

[22]This is as far as Hegel had gotten in revising the Preface before he died on November 14, 1831.

surface. Apprehending and proving consist similarly in seeing whether every one finds what is said corresponding to his idea too, whether it is familiar and seems to him so and so or not.

34. Analysis of an idea, as it used to be carried out, did in fact consist in nothing else than doing away with its character of familiarity. To break up an idea into its ultimate elements means returning upon its moments, which at least do not have the form of the given idea when found, but are the immediate property of the self. Doubtless this analysis only arrives at thoughts which are themselves familiar elements, fixed inert determinations. But what is thus separated, and in a sense is unreal, is itself an essential moment; for just because the concrete fact is self-divided, and turns into unreality, it is something self-moving, self-active. The action of separating the elements is the exercise of the force of Understanding, the most astonishing and greatest of all powers, or rather the absolute power. The circle, which is self-enclosed and at rest, and, *qua* substance, holds its own moments, is an immediate relation, the immediate, continuous relation of elements with their unity, and hence arouses no sense of wonderment. But that an accident as such, when cut loose from its containing circumference,—that what is bound and held by something else and actual only by being connected with it,—should obtain an existence all its own, gain freedom and independence on its own account—this is the portentous power of the negative; it is the energy of thought, of pure ego. Death, as we may call that unreality, is the most terrible thing, and to keep and hold fast what is dead demands the greatest force of all. Beauty, powerless and helpless, hates understanding, because the latter exacts from it what it cannot perform.[23] But the life of mind is not one that shuns death, and keeps clear of de-

---

[23]Baillie believes that this sentence is "directed against Novalis and the cult of Beauty." "Novalis" was the pseudonym of Friedrich Leopold Frieherr von Hardenberg (1772–1801), a great lyric poet, a leader among the early German romantics, and a follower of the philosopher Fichte (1762–1814).

struction; it endures death and in death maintains its being. It only wins to its truth when it finds itself utterly torn asunder.[24] It is this mighty power, not by being a positive which turns away from the negative, as when we say of anything it is nothing or it is false, and, being then done with it, pass off to something else: on the contrary, mind is this power only by looking the negative in the face, and dwelling with it. This dwelling beside it is the magic power that converts the negative into being. That power is just what we spoke of above as subject, which by giving determinateness a place in its substance, cancels abstract immediacy, i.e., immediacy which merely *is*, and, by so doing, becomes the true substance, becomes being or immediacy that does not have mediation outside it, but is this mediation itself.

35. This process of making what is objectively presented a possession of pure self-consciousness, of raising it to the level of universality in general, is merely one aspect of mental development; spiritual evolution is not yet completed. The manner of study in ancient times is distinct from that of the modern world, in that the former consisted in the cultivation and perfecting of the natural mind. Testing life carefully at all points, philosophizing about everything it came across, the former created an experience permeated through and through by universals.[25] In modern times, however, an individual finds

[24]This seems to allude to the rites associated with the Orphic Mysteries in ancient Greece. In these rites, the consuming of the body and blood of a dismembered bull or goat was intended to symbolically represent the suffering, death, and resurrection of the god Dionysus-Zagreus. See Sir James George Frazer, *The Golden Bough*, abridged ed. (New York: Macmillan, 1947), pp. 388–392. Also see n. 32 below.

[25]It was Socrates who, "in ancient times," devoted himself to uncovering the universal ideas, the common or general notes to be found in the particular details of experience, particularly moral experiences. Plato (428–348 B.C.) developed Socrates' views into a general theory, which held that the changing particulars of experience exist only because they participate in eternal and universal ideas, the εἶδος or *forms*.

the abstract form ready made.[26] In straining to grasp it and make it his own, he rather strives to bring forward the inner meaning alone, without any process of mediation; the production of the universal is abridged, instead of the universal arising out of the manifold detail of concrete existence. Hence nowadays the task before us consists not so much in getting the individual clear of the stage of sensuous immediacy, and making him a substance that thinks and is grasped in terms of thought, but rather the very opposite: it consists in actualizing the universal, and giving it spiritual vitality, by the process of breaking down and superseding fixed and determinate thoughts. But it is much more difficult to make fixed and definite thoughts fuse with one another and form a continuous whole than to bring sensuous existence into this state. The reason lies in what was said before. Thought determinations get their substance and the element of their existence from the ego, the power of the negative, or pure reality; while determinations of sense find this in impotent abstract immediacy, in mere being as such. Thoughts become fluent and interfuse, when thinking pure and simple, this inner immediacy, knows itself as a moment, when pure certainty of self abstracts from itself. It does not "abstract" in the sense of getting away from itself and setting itself on one side, but of surrendering the fixed quality of its self-affirmation, and giving up both the fixity of the purely concrete—which is the ego as contrasted with the variety of its content—and the fixity of all those distinctions [the various thought-functions, principles, etc.] which are present in the element of pure thought and share that absoluteness of the ego. In virtue of this process pure thoughts become notions, concepts, and are then what they are in truth, self-moving functions, circles, are what their substance consists in, are spiritual entities.

36. This movement of the spiritual entities constitutes the nature of scientific procedure in general. Looked at as the

---

[26]". . . abstract form ready made" alludes to Kant's theory of the *a priori* categories or forms that structure our experience.

concatenation of their content, this movement is the necessitated development and expansion of that content into an organic systematic whole. By this movement, too, the road, which leads to the notion of knowledge, becomes itself likewise a necessary and complete evolving process (*Werden*). This preparatory stage thus ceases to consist of casual philosophical reflections, referring to objects here and there, to processes and thoughts of the undeveloped mind as chance may direct; and it does not try to establish the truth by miscellaneous ratiocinations, inferences, and consequences drawn from circumscribed thoughts. The road to science, by the very movement of the notion itself, will compass the entire objective world of conscious life in its rational necessity.

37. Further, a systematic exposition like this constitutes the first part of science,[27] because the positive existence of mind, *qua* primary and ultimate, is nothing but the immediate aspect of mind, the beginning; the beginning, but not yet its return to itself. The characteristic feature distinguishing this part of science [Phenomenology] from the others is the element of positive immediate existence. The mention of this distinction leads us to discuss certain established ideas that usually come to notice in this connection.

38. The mind's immediate existence, conscious life, has two aspects—cognition and objectivity which is opposed to or negative of the subjective function of knowing. Since it is in the medium of consciousness that mind is developed and brings out its various moments, this opposition between the factors of conscious life is found at each stage in the evolution of mind, and all the various moments appear as modes or forms (*Gestalten*) of consciousness. The scientific statement of the course of this development is a science of the experience through which consciousness passes; the substance and its process are considered as the object of consciousness. Consciousness knows and comprehends nothing but what falls within its experience; for what is found in experience is

---

[27]See above, n. 21.

merely spiritual substance, and, moreover, object of its self. Mind, however, becomes object, for it consists in the process of becoming an other to itself, i.e., an object for its own self, and in transcending this otherness. And experience is called this very process by which the element that is immediate, unexperienced, i.e., abstract—whether it be in the form of sense or of a bare thought—externalizes itself, and then comes back to itself from this state of estrangement, and by so doing is at length set forth in its concrete nature and real truth, and becomes too a possession of consciousness.

39. The dissimilarity which obtains in consciousness between the ego and the substance constituting its object, is their inner distinction, the factor of negativity in general. We may regard it as the defect of both opposites, but it is their very soul, their moving spirit. It was on this account that certain thinkers[28] long ago took the void to be the principle of movement, when they conceived the moving principle to be the negative element, though they had not as yet thought of it as self. While this negative factor appears in the first instance as a dissimilarity, as an inequality, between ego and object, it is just as much the inequality of the substance with itself. What seems to take place outside it, to be an activity directed against it, is its own doing, its own activity; and substance shows that it is in reality subject. When it has brought out this completely, mind has made its existence adequate to and one with its essential nature. Mind is object to itself just as it *is*, and the abstract element of immediacy, of the separation between knowing and the truth, is overcome. Being is entirely mediated; it is a substantial content, that is likewise directly in the possession of the ego, has the character of self, is notion. With the attainment of this the Phenomenology of Mind concludes. What mind prepares for itself in the course of its phenomenol-

---

[28]The thinkers in question were the ancient Greek atomists, Leucippus and Democritus, who (in the fifth century B.C.) maintained that all things are composed of the smallest possible particles called "atoms," which in Greek means "indivisible." These atoms moved according to mechanical laws, without design, through the infinite void of space.

ogy is the element of true knowledge. In this element the moments of mind are now set out in the form of thought pure and simple, which knows its object to be itself. They no longer involve the opposition between being and knowing; they remain within the undivided simplicity of the knowing function; they are the truth in the form of truth, and their diversity is merely diversity of the content of truth. The process by which they are developed into an organically connected whole is Logic or Speculative Philosophy.

40. Now, because the systematic statement of the mind's experience embraces merely its ways of appearing, it may well seem that the advance from that to the science of ultimate truth in the form of truth is merely negative; and we might readily be content to dispense with the negative process as something altogether false, and might ask to be taken straight to the truth at once: why meddle with what is false at all? The point formerly raised, that we should have begun with science at once, may be answered here by considering the character of negativity in general regarded as something false. The usual ideas on this subject particularly obstruct the approach to the truth. The consideration of this point will give us an opportunity to speak about mathematical knowledge, which nonphilosophical knowledge looks upon as the ideal which philosophy ought to try to attain, but has so far striven in vain to reach.

41. Truth and falsehood as commonly understood belong to those sharply defined ideas which claim a completely fixed nature of their own, one standing in solid isolation on this side, the other on that, without any community between them. Against that view it must be pointed out, that truth is not like stamped coin[29] that is issued ready from the mint and

[29]A line from G. E. Lessing's (1729–1781) play *Nathan the Wise* (1779), act 3, sc. 5. Nathan, asked by the vizier Saladin to state which religion is true—Judaism, Islam, or Christianity—exclaims: "Truth. Truth! He wants it so—so ready-made, as if Truth were a coin!" Lessing was one of the most influential figures of the Enlightenment. Hegel often refers to him, especially in his *Early Theological Writings*.

so can be taken up and used. Nor, again, *is* there something false, any more than there *is* something evil. Evil and falsehood are indeed not so bad as the devil, for in the form of the devil they get the length of being particular subjects; *qua* false and evil they are merely universals, though they have a nature of their own with reference to one another. Falsity (that is what we are dealing with here) would be *otherness*, the negative aspect of the substance, which [substance], *qua* content of knowledge, is truth. But the substance is itself essentially the negative element, partly as involving distinction and determination of content, partly as being a process of distinguishing pure and simple, i.e., as being self and knowledge in general. Doubtless we can know in a way that is false. To know something falsely means that knowledge is not adequate to, is not on equal terms with, its substance. Yet this very dissimilarity is the process of distinction in general, the essential moment in knowing. It is, in fact, out of this active distinction that its harmonious unity arises, and this identity, when arrived at, is truth. But it is not truth in a sense which would involve the rejection of the discordance, the diversity, like dross from pure metal; nor, again, does truth remain detached from diversity, like a finished article from the instrument that shapes it. Difference itself continues to be an immediate element within truth as such, in the form of the principle of negation, in the form of the activity of Self. All the same, we cannot for that reason say that falsehood is a moment or forms even a constituent part of truth. That "in every case of falsity there is something true" is an expression in which they are taken to be like oil and water, which do not mix and are merely united externally. Just in the interest of their real meaning, precisely because we want to designate the aspect or moment of complete otherness, the terms true and false must no longer be used where their otherness has been cancelled and superseded. Just as the expressions "unity of subject and object," of "finite and infinite," of "being and thought," etc., are clumsy when subject and object, etc., are taken to mean what they are *outside* their unity, and are thus in that unity not meant to be what its very expression conveys; in the same way falsehood is not, *qua* false, any longer a moment of truth.

42. Dogmatism as a way of thinking, whether in ordinary knowledge or in the study of philosophy, is nothing else but the view that truth consists in a proposition, which is a fixed and final result, or again which is directly known. To questions like "When was Caesar born?", "How many feet make a furlong?", etc., a straight answer ought to be given; just as it is absolutely true that the square of the hypotenuse is equal to the sum of the squares of the other two sides of a right-angled triangle. But the nature of a so-called truth of that sort is different from the nature of philosophical truth.

43. As regards truth in matters of historical fact—to deal briefly with this subject—so far as we consider the purely historical element, it will be readily granted that they have to do with the sphere of particular existence, with a content in its contingent and arbitrary aspects, features that have no necessity. But even bare truths of the kind, say, like those mentioned, are impossible without the activity of self-consciousness. In order to know any one of them, there has to be a good deal of comparison, books must be consulted, or in some way or other inquiry has to be made. Even in a case of direct perception, only when we know it along with the reasons behind it, is it held to be something of real value; although it is merely the naked fact itself that we are, properly speaking, supposed to be concerned about.

44. As to mathematical truths, we should be still less inclined to consider anyone a geometer who had got Euclid's theorems[30] by heart (*auswendig*) without knowing the proofs, without, if we may say so by way of contrast, getting them into his head (*inwendig*). Similarly, if anyone came to know by

[30] The geometrical postulates (or axioms) and theorems (formulas deduced) in the *Elements* of Euclid, a Greek who wrote about 300 B.C., were regarded as unassailable until certain geometers in Hegel's day, unknowest to him, successfully challenged one of Euclid's postulates and developed non-Euclidian geometries.

measuring many right-angled triangles that their sides are related in the way everybody knows, we should regard knowledge so obtained as unsatisfactory. All the same, while proof is essential in the case of mathematical knowledge, it still does not have the significance and nature of being a moment in the result itself; the proof is over when we get the result, and has disappeared. *Qua* result the theorem is, no doubt, one that is seen to be true. But this eventuality has nothing to do with its content, but only with its relation to the knowing subject. The process of mathematical proof does not belong to the object; it is a function that takes place outside the matter in hand. Thus, the nature of a right-angled triangle does not break itself up into factors in the manner set forth in the mathematical construction which is required to prove the proposition expressing the relation of its parts. The entire process of producing the result is an affair of knowledge which takes its own way of going about it. In philosophical knowledge, too, the way existence, *qua* existence, comes about (*Werden*) is different from that whereby the essence or inner nature of the fact comes into being. But philosophical knowledge, for one thing, contains both, while mathematical knowledge sets forth merely the way an existence comes about, i.e., the way the nature of the fact gets to *be* in the sphere of knowledge as such. For another thing, too, philosophical knowledge unites both these particular movements. The inward rising into being, the process of substance, is an unbroken transition into outwardness, into existence or being for another; and conversely, the coming of existence into being is withdrawal into the inner essence. The movement is the twofold process in which the whole comes to be, and is such that each at the same time posits the other, and each on that account has in it both as its two aspects. Together they make the whole, through their resolving each other, and making themselves into moments of the whole.

45. In mathematical knowledge the insight required is an external function so far as the subject-matter dealt with is concerned. It follows that the actual fact is thereby altered.

The means taken, construction and proof, contain, no doubt, true propositions; but all the same we are bound to say that the content is false. The triangle in the above example is taken to pieces, and its parts made into other figures to which the construction in the triangle gives rise. It is only at the end that we find again reinstated the triangle we are really concerned with; it was lost sight of in the course of the construction, and was present merely in fragments, that belonged to other wholes. Thus we find negativity of content coming in here too, a negativity of content coming in here too, a negativity which would have to be called falsity, just as much as in the case of the movement of the notion where thoughts that are taken to be fixed pass away and disappear.

46. The real defect of this kind of knowledge, however, affects its process of knowing as much as its material. As to that process, in the first place we do not see any necessity in the construction. The necessity does not arise from the nature of the theorem: it is imposed; and the injunction to draw just these lines, an infinite number of others being equally possible, is blindly acquiesced in, without our knowing anything further, except that, as we fondly believe, this will serve our purpose in producing the proof. Later on this design then comes out too, and is therefore merely external in character, just because it is only after the proof is found that it comes to be known. In the same way, again, the proof takes a direction that begins anywhere we like, without our knowing as yet what relation this beginning has to the result to be brought out. In its course, it takes up certain specific elements and relations and lets others alone, without its being directly obvious what necessity there is in the matter. An external purpose controls this process.

47. The evidence peculiar to this defective way of knowing—an evidence on the strength of which mathematics plumes itself and proudly struts before philosophy—rests solely on the poverty of its purpose and the defectiveness of its material, and is on that account of a kind that philosophy must scorn to have anything to do with. Its purpose or principle is quantity. This

is precisely the relationship that is non-essential, alien to the character of the notion. The process of knowledge goes on, therefore, on the surface, does not affect the concrete fact itself, does not touch its inner nature or notion, and is hence not a conceptual way of comprehending. The material which provides mathematics with these welcome treasures of truth consists of space and numerical units (*das Eins*). Space is that kind of existence wherein the concrete notion inscribes the diversity it contains, as in an empty, lifeless element in which its differences likewise subsist in passive, lifeless form. What is concretely actual is not something spatial, such as is treated of in mathematics. With unrealities like the things mathematics takes account of, neither concrete sensuous perception nor philosophy has anything to do. In an unreal element of that sort we find, then, only unreal truth, fixed lifeless propositions. We can call a halt at any of them; the next begins of itself *de novo*, without the first having led up to the one that follows, and without any necessary connection having in this way arisen from the nature of the subject-matter itself. So, too—and herein consists the formal character of mathematical evidence—because of that principle and the element where it applies, knowledge advances along the lines of bare equality, of abstract identity. For what is lifeless, not being self-moved, does not bring about distinction within its essential nature; does not attain to essential opposition or unlikeness; and hence involves no transition of one opposite element into its other, no qualitative, immanent movement, no *self*-movement, It is quantity, a form of difference that does not touch the essential nature, which alone mathematics deals with. It abstracts from the fact that it is the notion which separates space into its dimensions, and determines the connexions between them and in them. It does not consider, for example, the relation of line to surface, and when it compares the diameter of a circle with its circumference, it runs up against their incommensurability, i.e., a relation in terms of the notion, an infinite element, that escapes mathematical determination.

48. Immanent or so-called pure mathematics, again, does

not oppose time *qua* time to space, as a second subject-matter for consideration. Applied mathematics, no doubt, treats of time, as also of motion, and other concrete things as well; but it picks up from experience synthetic propositions—i.e., statements of their relations, which are determined by their conceptual nature—and merely applies its formulae to those propositions assumed to start with. That the so-called proofs of propositions like that concerning the equilibrium of the lever, the relation of space and time in gravitation, etc., which applied mathematics frequently gives, should be taken and given as proofs, is itself merely a proof of how great the need is for knowledge to have a process of proof, seeing that, even where proof is not to be had, knowledge yet puts a value on the mere semblance of it, and gets thereby a certain sense of satisfaction. A criticism of those proofs would be as instructive as it would be significant, if the criticism could strip mathematics of this artificial finery, and bring out its limitations, and thence show the necessity for another type of knowledge.

49. As to time, which, it is to be presumed, would, by way of the counterpart to space, constitute the object-matter of the other division of pure mathematics, this is the notion itself in the form of existence. The principle of quantity, of difference which is not determined by the notion, and the principle of equality, of abstract, lifeless unity, are incapable of dealing with that sheer restlessness of life and its absolute and inherent process of differentiation. It is therefore only in an arrested, paralyzed form, only in the form of the quantitative unit, that this essentially negative activity becomes the second object-matter of this way of knowing, which, itself an external operation, degrades what is self-moving to the level of mere matter, in order thus to get an indifferent, external, lifeless content.[31]

[31]A very similar critique of mathematical attempts to represent time flow played a central role in the philosophy of Henri Bergson (1859–1941). (See *Creative Evolution* [New York: Modern Library, 1944], pp. 11–13).

50. Philosophy, on the contrary, does not deal with a determination that is non-essential, but with a determination so far as it is an essential factor. The abstract or unreal is not its element and content, but the real, what is self-establishing, has life within itself, existence in its very notion. It is the process that creates its own moments in its course, and goes through them all; and the whole of this movement constitutes its positive content and its truth. This movement includes, therefore, within it the negative factor as well, the element which would be named falsity if it could be considered one from which we had to abstract. The element that disappears has rather to be looked at as itself essential, not in the sense of being something fixed, that has to be cut off from truth and allowed to lie outside it, heaven knows where; just as similarly the truth is not to be held to stand on the other side as an immovable lifeless positive element. Appearance is the process of arising into being and passing away again, a process that itself does not arise and does not pass away, but is *per se*, and constitutes reality and the life-movement of truth. The truth is thus the bacchanalian revel, where not a member is sober; and because every member no sooner becomes detached than it *eo ipso* collapses straightway, the revel is just as much a state of transparent unbroken calm.[32] Judged by that movement, the particular shapes which mind assumes do not indeed subsist

[32]*Die Wahre is so der bacchantische Taumel . . .* The Bacchanalia of ancient Roman times were drunken orgies associated with the cult of the god Bacchus (Dionysus [see n. 21 above]) under his aspect as the riotious god of wine). In 186 B.C. the Roman senate banned the Bacchanalia on account of their extreme licentiousness. (See Martin Leach, ed., *Standard Dictionary of Folklore, Mythology, and Legend* [New York: Funk & Wagnalls, 1949], s.v.. "Bacchus.") Later, in the main body of the *Phenomenology*, Hegel says that those who seek truth in the objects of sense should "be sent back to the most elementary school of wisdom, the ancient Eleusinian mysteries of Ceres and Bacchus . . ." wherein candidates for initiation acknowledged the transitory and insubstantial character of sensual things by consuming and destroying representative examples of them, such as bread and wine. See Baillie trans., p. 159.

any more than do determinate thoughts or ideas; but they are, all the same, as much positive and necessary moments, as negative and transitory. In the entirety of the movement, taken as an unbroken quiescent whole, that which obtains distinctness in the course of its process and secures specific existence, is preserved in the form of a self-recollection, in which existence is self-knowledge, and self-knowledge, again, is immediate existence.

51. It might well seem necessary to state at the outset the chief points in connection with the *method* of this process, the way in which science operates. Its nature, however, is to be found in what has already been said, while the proper systematic exposition of it is the special business of Logic, or rather is Logic itself. For the method is nothing else than the structure of the whole in its pure and essential form. In regard, however, to what has been hitherto currently held on this point, we must be sensible that the system of ideas bearing on the question of philosophical method, belongs also to a stage of mental culture that has now passed away. This may perhaps seem somewhat boastful or revolutionary; and I am far from adopting an attitude of that sort; but it is significant that the scientific régime bequeathed by mathematics—a régime of explanations, divisions, axioms, an array of theorems, with proofs, principles, and the consequences and conclusions drawn from them—all this has already come to be generally considered as at any rate out of date. Even though there is no clear idea why it is unsuitable, yet little or no use is made of it any longer; and even though it is not condemned outright, it is all the same not in favor. And we must be so far prejudiced in favor of what is excellent to believe that it can turn itself to practical account, and make itself acceptable. But it is not difficult to see that the method of propounding a proposition, producing reasons for it and then refuting its opposite by reasons too, is not the form in which truth can appear. Truth moves itself by its very nature; but the method just mentioned is a form of knowledge external to its material. Hence it is peculiar to mathematics and must be left to mathematics,

which, as already indicated, takes for its principle the relation
of quantity, a relation alien to the notion, and gets its material
from lifeless space, and the equally lifeless numerical unit. Or,
again, such a method, adopting a freer style, one involving
more of arbitrariness and chance, may have a place in ordinary
life, in a conversation, or in supplying matter-of-fact instruction for the satisfaction of curiosity rather than knowledge,
very much as a preface does. In everyday life the mind finds
its content in different kinds of knowledge, experiences of
various sorts, concrete facts of sense, thoughts, too, and principles, and, in general, in whatever lies ready to hand, or
passes for a solid stable entity, or real being. The mind follows
wherever this leads, sometimes interrupting the connection
by an unrestrained caprice in dealing with the content, and
takes up the attitude of determining and handling it in quite an
external fashion. It runs the content back to some touchstone
of certainty or other, even though it be but the feeling of the
moment; and conviction is satisfied if it reaches some familiar
resting-place.

52. But when the necessity of the notion banishes from its
realm the loose procedure of the "raisonnements" of conversation, as well as the pedantic style of scientific pomposity, its
place, as we have already mentioned, must not be taken by the
disconnected utterance of presageful surmise and inspiration,[33] and the arbitrary caprice of prophetic utterance; for
this does not merely despise that particular form of scientific
procedure, but contemns scientific procedure altogether.

53. Now that the triplicity, adopted in the system of Kant[34]
—a method rediscovered, to begin with, by instinctive insight,

---

[33]*Nicht durch die Unmethode des Ahnens und der Begeisterung* . . .
Ahnens "presageful surmise" in this context suggests that Hegel had in
mind the work of Jakob F. Fries (1773–1843): *Wissen, Glaube und
Ahnung (Knowledge, Faith, and Surmise)*. Hegel, in his *Philosophy of
Right*, described Fries thought as "the quintessence of shallow thinking."

[34]As, for example, the Table of Categories presented by Kant in the
Critique of Pure Reason, B. 106.

but left lifeless and uncomprehended has been raised to its significance as an absolute method, true form is thereby set up in its true content, and the conception of science has come to light. But the use this form has been put to in certain quarters has no right to the name of science. For we see it there reduced to a lifeless schema, to nothing better than a mere shadow, and scientific organization to a synoptic table. This formalism—about which we spoke before in general terms, and whose procedure we wish here to state more fully— thinks it has comprehended and expressed the nature and life of a given form when it proclaims a determination of the schema to be its predicate. The predicate may be subjectivity or objectivity, or again magnetism, electricity, and so on, contraction or expansion, East or West, and such like—a form of predication that can be multiplied indefinitely, because according to this way of working each determination, each mode, can be applied as a form or schematic element in the case of every other, and each will thankfully perform the same service for any other. With a circle of reciprocities of this sort it is impossible to make out what the real fact in question is, or what the one or the other is. We find there sometimes constituents of sense picked up from ordinary intution, determinate elements which to be sure should mean something else than they say; at other times what is inherently significant, viz. pure determinations of thought—like subject, object, substance, cause, universality, etc.—these are applied just as uncritically and unreflectingly as in everyday life, are used much as people employ the terms strong and weak, expansion and contraction. As a result that type of metaphysics is as unscientific as those ideas of sense.

54. Instead of the inner activity and self-movement of its own actual life, such a simple determination of direct intuition (*Anschauung*)—which means here sense-knowledge—is predicated in accordance with a superficial analogy, and this external and empty application of the formula is called "construction." The same thing happens here, however, as in the case of every kind of formalism. A man's head must be indeed

dull if he could not in a quarter of an hour get up the theory[35] that there are enervating, innervating, and indirectly enervating diseases and as many cures, and who could not—since not so long ago instruction of that sort sufficed for the purpose— in as short a time be turned from being a man who works by rule of thumb into a theoretical physician. Formalism in the case of speculative Philosophy of Nature (*Naturphilosophie*) takes the shape of teaching that understanding is electricity, animals are nitrogen, or equivalent to South or North and so on. When it does this, whether as badly as it is here expressed or even concocted with more terminology, such forceful procedure brings and holds together elements to all appearance far removed from one another; the violence done to stable inert sense-elements by connecting them in this way, confers on them merely the semblance of a conceptual unity, and spares itself the trouble of doing what is after all the important thing—expressing the notion itself, the meaning that underlies sense-ideas. All this sort of thing may strike anyone who has no experience with admiration and wonder. He may be awed by the profound genius he thinks it displays, and be delighted at the happy ingenuity of such characterizations, since they fill the place of the abstract notion with something tangible and sensuous, and so make it more pleasing; and he may congratulate himself on feeling an instinctive mental affinity for that glorious way of proceeding. The trick of wisdom of that sort is as quickly acquired as it is easy to practice. Its repetition, when once it is familiar, becomes as boring as the repetition of any bit of sleight-of-hand once we see through it. The instrument for producing this monotonous formalism is no more

[35]An indirect reference to the *Elementa medicinae* (1780) of the Scottish physician John Brown (1735–1788). Brown was a popular promoter of the "excitability" theory of medicine, which classified diseases according to whether they had an over- or understimulating effect on the body. Hegel had heard of the sensational and rambunctious two-day debate between "Brownians" and "anti-Brownians" that occurred in 1802 at the University of Göttingen.

difficult to handle than the palette of a painter, on which lie
only two colors, say red and green, the former for coloring the
surface when we want a historical piece, the latter when we
want a bit of landscape. It would be difficult to settle which is
greater in all this, the agreeable ease with which everything in
heaven and earth and under the earth is plastered with that
botch of color, or the conceit that prides itself on the excellence of its means for every conceivable purpose; the one
lends support to the other. What results from the use of this
method of sticking on to everything in heaven and earth, to
every kind of shape and form, natural and spiritual, the pair of
determinations from the general schema, and filing everything
in this manner, is no less than an "account as clear as noonday"[36] of the organized whole of the universe. It is, that is to
say, a synoptic index, like a skeleton with tickets stuck all over
it, or like the rows of boxes kept shut and labelled in a grocer's
stall; and is as intelligible as either the one or the other. It has
lost hold of the living nature of concrete fact; just as in the
former case we have merely dry bones with flesh and blood
all gone, and in the latter, there is shut away in those boxes
something equally lifeless too. We have already remarked that
the final outcome of this style of thinking is, at the same time,
to paint entirely in one kind of color; for it turns with contempt from the distinctions in the schematic table, looks on
them as belonging to the activity of mere reflection, and lets
them drop out of sight in the void of the Absolute, and there
reinstates pure identity, pure formless whiteness.[37] Such uniformity of coloring in the schema with its lifeless determina-

---

[36]A phrase from Fichte's *An Account as Clear as Noonday to the
Public at Large about the True Nature of The Newest Philosophy* [*Son-
nenklarer Bericht an das Publikum über das eigentliche Wesen der
neuesten Philosophie, 1801*]. Fichte wrote this work in rebuttal of crit-
icisms that he regarded as greviously misrepresenting his philosophy.

[37]This is another remarkable image critical of Schelling's school, but
one quite opposite from the previous one. Here, in the "void of the
Absolute," all is white, whereas before all was black. See above, n.11.

tions, this absolute identity, and the transition from one to the other—these are the one as well as the other, the expression of inert lifeless understanding, and equally an external process of knowledge.

55. Not only can what is excellent not escape the fate of being thus devitalized and despiritualized and excoriated of seeing its skin paraded about by lifeless knowledge and the conceit such knowledge engenders; but rather, such a fate lets us realize the power the "excellent" exercises over the heart (*Gemüth*), if not over the mind (*Geist*). Moreover, we recognize thereby, too, the constructive unfolding into universality and determinateness of form which marks the complete attainment of excellence, and which alone makes it possible that this universality can be turned to superficial uses.

56. Science can become an organic system only by the inherent life of the notion. In science the determinateness, which was taken from the schema and stuck on to existing facts in external fashion, is the self-directing inner soul of the concrete content. The movement of what is partly consists in becoming another to itself, and thus developing explicitly into its own immanent content; partly, again, it takes this evolved content, this existence it assumes, back into itself, i.e., makes *itself* into a moment, and reduces itself to simple determinateness. In the first stage of the process negativity lies in the function of distinguishing and establishing existence; in this latter return into self, negativity consists in the bringing about of determinate simplicity. It is in this way that the content shows its specific characteristic not to be received from something else, and stuck on externally; the content gives itself this determinate characteristic, appoints itself of its own initiative to the rank of a moment and to a place in the whole. The pigeon-holing process of understanding retains for itself the necessity and the notion controlling the content, that which constitutes the concrete element, the actuality and living process of the subject-matter which it labels: or rather, understanding does not retain this for itself, on the contrary, understanding fails to know it. For if it had as much insight as that, it

would surely show that it had. It is not even aware of the need for such insight; if it were, it would drop its schematizing process, or at least would no longer be satisfied to know by way of a mere table of contents. A table of contents is all that understanding gives, the content itself it does not furnish at all.

57. If the specific determination (say even one like magnetism) is one that in itself is concrete or actual, it all the same gets degraded into something lifeless and inert, since it is merely predicated of another existing entity, and not known as an immanent living principle of this existence; nor is there any comprehension of how in this entity its intrinsic and peculiar way of expressing and producing itself takes effect. This, the very kernel of the matter, formal understanding leaves to others to add later on. Instead of making its way into the inherent content of the matter in hand, understanding always takes a survey of the whole, assumes a position above the particular existence about which it is speaking, i.e., it does not see it at all. True scientific knowledge, on the contrary, demands abandonment to the very life of the object, or, which means the same thing, claims to have before it the inner necessity controlling the object, and to express this only. Steeping itself in its object, it forgets to take that general survey, which is merely a turning of knowledge away from the content back into itself. But being sunk into the material in hand, and following the course that such material takes, true knowledge returns back into itself, yet not before the content in its fullness is taken into itself, is reduced to the simplicity of being a determinate characteristic, drops to the level of being one aspect of an existing entity, and passes over into its higher truth. By this process the whole as such, surveying its entire content, itself emerges out of the wealth wherein its process of reflection seemed to be lost.

58. In general, in virtue of the principle that, as we expressed it before, substance is implicitly and in itself subject, all content makes its reflection into itself in its own special way. The subsistence or substance of anything that exists is its self-identity; for its want of identity, or oneness with itself,

would be its dissolution. But self-identity is pure abstraction; and this is just thinking. When I say Quality, I state simple determinateness; by means of its quality one existence is distinguished from another or is an "existence"; it is for itself, something on its own account, or subsists with itself because of this simple characteristic. But by doing so it is essentially Thought.

59. Here we find contained the principle that Being is Thought[38] here is exercised that insight which usually tends to deviate from the ordinary non-conceptual way of speaking of the identity of thought and being. In virtue, further, of the fact that subsistence on the part of what exists is self-identity or pure abstraction, it is the abstraction of itself from itself, in other words, is itself its own want of identity with itself and dissolution—its own proper inwardness and retraction into self—its process of becoming.

60. Owing to the nature which being thus has, and so far as what is has this nature from the point of view of knowledge, this thinking is not an activity which treats the content as something alien and external; it is not reflection into self away from the content. Science is not that kind of Idealism which stepped into the place of the Dogmatism of mere assertion and took the shape of a Dogmatism of mere assurance, the Dogmatism of mere self-certainty. Rather, since knowledge sees the content go back into its own proper inner nature, the activity of knowledge is absorbed in that content—for it (the activity) is the immanent self of the content—and is also at the same time returned into itself, for this activity is pure self-identity in otherness. In this way the knowing activity is the artful device which, while seeming to refrain from activity, looks on and watches how specific determinateness with its concrete life, just where it believes it is working out its own self-preservation and its own private interest, is, in point of fact, doing the

[38]A doctrine held, as Hegel interprets him, by Parmenides. Hegel regards Parmenides as the main forerunner of Spinoza.

very opposite, is doing what brings about its own dissolution and makes itself a moment in the whole.

61. While, in the foregoing, the significance of Understanding was stated from the point of view of the self-consciousness of substance; by what has been here stated we can see clearly its significance from the point of view of substance *qua* being. Existence is Quality, self-identical determinateness, or determinate simplicity, determinate thought: this is existence from the point of view of Understanding. On this account it is νοῦς, as Anaxagoras[39] first thought reality to be. Those who succeeded him grasped the nature of existence in a more determinate way as εἶδος or ιδέα,[40] i.e., as determinate or specific universality, kind or species. The term species or kind seems indeed too ordinary and inadequate for Ideas, for beauty, holiness, eternal, which are the vogue in these days. As a matter of fact, however, idea (ιδέα) means neither more nor less than kind, species. But we often find nowadays that a term which exactly designates a conception is despised and rejected, and another preferred to it which hides and obscures the conception, and thus sounds more edifying, even though this is merely due to its being expressed in a foreign language.

62. Precisely for the reason that existence is designated a species or kind, it is a naked simple thought; νοῦς, simplicity, is substance. It is on account of its simplicity, its self-identity, that it appears steady, fixed, and permanent. But this self-identity is likewise negativity; hence that fixed and stable existence carries the process of its own dissolution within itself. The determinateness appears at first to be so solely through its relation to something else; and its process seems imposed and forced upon it externally. But its having its own otherness within itself, and the fact of its being a self-initiated

---

[39]The Greek philosopher Anaxagoras (about 500–428 B.C.), argued in his book *On Nature* that "Mind" or "Reason" (νοῦς) governs the disposition of matter in the universe.

[40]Plato gave philosophical significance and currency to the terms εἶδος (eidos), usually translated as "Form" and ιδέα ("Idea"). See above, n. 25.

process—these are implied in the very simplicity of thought itself. For this is self-moving thought, thought that distinguishes, is inherent inwardness, the pure notion. Thus, then, it is the very nature of understanding to be a process; and being a process it is Rationality.

63. In the nature of existence as thus described—to be its own notion and being in one—consists logical necessity in general. This alone is what is rational, the rhythm of the organic whole: it is as much knowledge of content as that content is notion and essential nature. In other words, this alone is the sphere and element of speculative thought. The concrete shape of the content is resolved by its own inherent process into a simple determinate quality. Thereby it is raised to logical form, and its being and essence coincide; its concrete existence is merely this process that takes place, and is *eo ipso* logical existence. It is therefore needless to apply a formal scheme to the concrete content in an external fashion; the content is in its very nature a transition into a formal shape, which, however, ceases to be formalism of an external kind, because the form is the indwelling process of the concrete content itself.

64. This nature of scientific method, which consists partly in being inseparable from the content, and partly in determining the rhythm of its movement by its own agency, finds, as we mentioned before, its peculiar systematic expression in speculative philosophy. What is here stated describes in effect the essential principle; but cannot stand for more at this stage than an assertion or assurance by way of anticipation. The truth it contains is not to be found in this exposition, which is in part historical in character. And just for that reason, too, it is not in the least refuted if anyone assures us on the contrary that this is not so, that the process instead is here so and so; if ideas we are all used to, being truths accepted or settled and familiar to everyone, are brought to mind and recounted; or, again, if something new is served up and guaranteed as coming from the inner sanctuaries of inspired intuition.

65. Such a view is bound to meet with opposition. The first instinctive reaction on the part of knowing, when offered something that was unfamiliar, is usually to resist it. It seeks by that means to save freedom and native insight, to secure its own inherent authority—against alien authority—for that is the way anything apprehended for the first time appears. This attitude is adopted, too, in order to do away with the semblance of a kind of disgrace which would lie in the fact that something has had to be learnt. In like manner, again, when the unfamiliar or unknown is received with applause, the reaction is in the same way an exaltation of freedom and native authority. It consists in something analogous to ultra-revolutionary declamation and action.[41]

66. Hence the important thing for the student of science is to make himself undergo the strenuous toil of conceptual reflection, of thinking in the form of the notion. This demands concentrated attention on the notion as such, on simple and ultimate determinations like being-in-itself, being-for-itself, self-identity, and so on; for these are elemental, pure, self-determined functions of a kind we might call souls, were it not that their conceptual nature denotes something higher than that term contains. The interruption by conceptual thought of the habit of always thinking in figurative ideas (*Vorstellungen*) is as annoying and troublesome to this way of thinking as to that process of formal intelligence which in its reasoning rambles about with no real thoughts to reason with. The former, the habit, may be called materialized thinking, a fortuitous mental state, one that is absorbed in what is material, and hence finds it very distasteful at once to lift its self clear of this matter and be with itself alone. The latter, the process of *raisonnement*, is, on the other hand, detachment from all content, and conceited superiority to it. What is wanted here is the effort and struggle to give up this kind of freedom, and

[41]The term "ultra-revolutionary" was used during the French Revolution to describe the most radical of the political clubs.

instead of being a merely arbitrary principle directing the content anyhow, this freedom should sink into and pervade the content, should let it be directed and controlled by its own proper nature, i.e., by the self as its own self, and should observe this process taking place. We must abstain from interrupting the immanent rhythm of the movement of conceptual thought; we must refrain from arbitrarily interfering with it, and introducing ideas and reflections that have been obtained elsewhere. Restraint of this sort is itself an essential condition of attending to and getting at the real nature of the notion.

67. There are two aspects in the case of that ratiocinative procedure which mark its contrast from conceptual thinking and call for further notice. *Raisonnement*, in the first place, adopts a negative attitude towards the content apprehended; knows how to refute it and reduce it to nothingness. To see what the content is *not* is merely a negative process; it is a dead halt, which does not of itself go beyond itself, and proceed to a new content; it has to get hold of something else from somewhere or other in order to have once more a content. It is reflection upon and into the empty ego, the vanity of its own knowledge. Conceit of this kind brings out not only that this content is vain and empty, but also that to see this is itself fatuity too: for it is negation with no perception of the positive element within it. In that this reflection does not even have its own negativity as its content, it is not inside actual fact at all, but for ever away outside it. On that account it imagines that by asserting mere emptiness it is going much farther than insight that embraces and reveals a wealth of content. On the other hand, in the case of conceptual thinking, as was above indicated, the negative aspect falls within the content itself, and is the positive substance of that content, as well as being its inherent character and moving principle as by being the entirety of what these are. Looked at as a result, it is determinate specific negation, the negative which is the outcome of this process, and consequently is a positive content as well.

68. In view of the fact that ratiocinative thinking has a content, whether of images or thoughts or a mixture of both,

there is another side to its process which makes conceptual comprehension difficult for it. The peculiar nature of this aspect is closely connected with the essential meaning of the idea above described, in fact, expresses the idea in the way this appears as the process of thinking apprehension. For just as ratiocinative thinking in its negative reference, which we have been describing, is nothing but the self into which the content returns; in the same way, on the other hand, in its positive cognitive process the self is an ideally presented subject to which the content is related as an accident and predicate. This subject constitutes the basis to which the content is attached and on which the process moves to and fro. Conceptual thinking goes on in quite a different way. Since the concept or notion is the very self of the object, manifesting itself as the development of the object, is is not a quiescent subject, passively supporting accidents: it is a self-determining active concept which takes up its determinations and makes them its own. In the course of this process that inert passive subject really disappears; it enters into the different constituents and pervades the content; instead of remaining in inert antithesis to determinateness of content, it constitutes, in fact, that very specificity, i.e., the content as differentiated along with the process of bringing this about. Thus the solid basis, which ratiocination found in an inert subject, is shaken to its foundations, and the only object is this very movement of the subject. The subject supplying the concrete filling to its own content ceases to be something transcending this content, and cannot have further predicates or accidents. Conversely, again, the scattered diversity of the content is brought under the control of the self, and so bound together; the content is not a universal that can be detached from the subject, and adapted to several indifferently. Consequently the content is in truth no longer predicate of the subject; it is the very substance, is the inmost reality, and the very principle of what is being considered. Ideational thinking (*vorstellen*), since its nature consists in dealing with accidents or predicates, and in exercising the right to transcend them because they are nothing more than predicates and accidents—this way of thinking is checked in its course, since that which has in the proposition the form of a predicate is itself the substance of the statement. It is met by a counter-thrust, as we may say. Starting from the subject, as if this were a permanent base on which to proceed, it discovers, by the predicate being in reality the substance, that the subject has passed into the predicate, and has thereby ceased to be subject: and since in this way what seems to be predicate has become the entire mass of the content, whole and complete, thinking cannot wander and ramble about at will, but is restrained and controlled by this weight of content.

69. Usually the subject is first set down as the fixed and objective self; from this fixed position the necessary process passes on to the multiplicity of determinations or predicates. Here the knowing ego takes the place of that subject and is the function of knitting or combining the predicates one with another, and is the subject holding them fast. But since the former subject enters into the determinate constituents themselves, and is their very life, the subject in the second case— viz. the knowing subject—finds that the former,—which it is supposed to be done with and which it wants to transcend, in order to return into itself,—is still there in the predicate: and instead of being able to be the determining agency in the process of resolving the predicate—reflectively deciding whether this or that predicate should be attached to the former subject—it has really to deal with the self of the content, is not allowed to be something on its own account (*für sich*), but has to exist along with this content.

70. What has been said can be expressed in a formal manner by saying that the nature of judgment or the proposition in general, which involves the distinction of subject and predicate, is subverted and destroyed by the speculative judgment; and the identical proposition, which the former becomes [by uniting subject and predicate], implies the rejection and repudiation of the above relation between subject and predicate. This conflict between the form of a proposition in general and

the unity of the notion which destroys that form, is similar to what we find between metre and accent in the case of rhythm. Rhythm is the result of what hovers between and unites both. So in the case of the speculative or philosophical judgment; the identity of subject and predicate is not intended to destroy their distinction, as expressed in propositional form; their unity is to arise as a harmony of the elements. The form of the judgment is the way the specific sense appears, or is made manifest, the accent which differentiates the meaning it contains: that the predicate expresses the substance, and the subject itself falls within the universal, is however the unity wherein that accent dies away.

71. To explain what has been said by examples let us take the proposition God is Being. The predicate is "being": it has substantive significance, and thus absorbs the meaning of the subject within it. Being is meant to be here not predicate but the essential nature. Thereby, God seems to cease to be what he was when the proposition was put forward, viz. a fixed subject. Thinking [i.e., ordinary reflection], instead of getting any farther with the transition from subject to predicate, in reality finds its activity checked through the loss of the subject, and it is thrown back on the thought of the subject because it misses this subject. Or again, since the predicate has itself been pronounced to be a subject, to be *the* being, to be the essential reality, which exhausts the nature of the subject, thinking finds the subject directly present in the predicate too: and now, instead of having, in the predicate, gone into *itself*, and preserved the freedom characteristic of ratiocination, it is absorbed in the content all the while, or, at any rate is required to be so.

72. Similarly, when it is said: "the real is the universal," the real, *qua* subject, passes away in its predicate. The universal is not only meant to have the significance of a predicate, as if the proposition stated that the real is universal: the universal is meant to express the essential nature of the real. Thinking therefore loses that fixed objective basis which it had in the

subject, just as much as in the predicate it is thrown back on the subject, and therein returns not into itself but into the subject underlying the content.

73. This unaccustomed restraint imposed upon thought is for the most part the cause of the complaints concerning the unintelligibility of philosophical writings, when otherwise the individual has in him the requisite mental cultivation for understanding them. In what has been said we see the reason for the specific charge often made against them, that a good deal has to be read repeatedly before it can be understood—an accusation which is meant to convey something improper in the extreme, and one which if granted to be sound admits of no further reply. It is obvious from the above what is the state of the case here. The philosophical proposition, being a proposition, calls up the accepted view of the usual relation of subject and predicate, and suggests the idea of the customary procedure which takes place in knowledge. Its philosophical content destroys this way of proceeding and the ordinary view taken of this process. The common view discovers that the statement is intended in another sense than it is thinking of, and this correction of its opinion compels knowledge to recur to the proposition and take it now in some other sense.

74. There is a difficulty which might well be avoided. It consists in mixing up the methods of procedure followed by speculation and ratiocination, when what is said of the subject has at one time the significance of its conceptual principle, and at another time the meaning of its predicate or accidental quality. The one mode of thinking invalidates the other; and only that philosophical exposition can manage to become plastic in character which resolutely sets aside and has nothing to do with the ordinary way of relating the parts of a proposition.

75. As a matter of fact, non-speculative thinking has its rights too, which are justifiable, but are disregarded in the speculative way of stating a proposition. Abolishing the form of the proposition must not take place only in an immediate manner, through the mere content of the proposition. On the

contrary, we must give explicit expression to this cancelling process; it must be not only that internal restraining and confining of thought within its own substance; this turning of the conception back into itself has to be expressly brought out and stated. This process, which constitutes what formerly had to be accomplished by proof, is the internal dialectical movement of the proposition itself. This alone is the concrete speculative element, and only the explicit expression of this is a speculative systematic exposition. *Qua* proposition, the speculative aspect is merely the internal restriction of thought within its own substance where the return of the essential principle into itself is not yet brought out. Hence we often find philosophical expositions referring us to the inner intuition, and thus dispensing with the systematic statement of the dialectical movement of the proposition, which is what we wanted all the while. The proposition ought to express *what* the truth is: in its essential nature the truth is subject: being so, it is merely the dialectical movement, this self-producing course of activity, maintaining its advance by returning back into itself. In the case of knowledge in other spheres this aspect of expressly stating the internal nature of the content is constituted by proof. When dialectic, however, has been separated from proof, the idea of philosophical demonstration as a matter of fact has vanished altogether.

76. On this point it may be mentioned that the dialectical process likewise consists of parts or elements which are propositions. The difficulty indicated seems therefore to recur continually, and seems to be a difficulty inherent in the nature of the case. This is like what happens in the ordinary process of proving anything; the grounds it makes use of need themselves to be based on other grounds again, and so on *ad infinitum*. This manner of furnishing grounds and conditions, however, concerns that type of proof from which the dialectical movement is distinct and hence belongs to the process of external knowledge. As to what this movement is, its element is the bare concept; this furnishes a content which is through and through subject *impliciter* and *per se*. There is to be

found, therefore, no sort of content standing in a relation, as it were, to an underlying subject, and getting its significance by being attached to this as a predicate. The proposition as it appears is a mere empty form.

77. Apart from the sensuously apprehended or ideally presented (*vorgestellten*) self, it is in the main the mere name *qua* name which denotes the subject pure and simple, the empty unit without any conceptual character. For this reason it would, e.g., be expedient to avoid the name "God," because this word is not in its primary use a conception as well, but the special name of an underlying subject, its fixed resting-place; while, on the other hand, being or the one, singleness, subject, etc., themselves directly indicate conceptions. Furthermore, if speculative truths are stated about that subject [God], even then their content is devoid of the immanent notion, because that content is merely present in the form of a passive subject, and owing to this the speculative truths easily take on the character of mere edification. From this side, too, the obstacle, arising from the habit of putting the speculative predicate in the form of a proposition, instead of taking it as an inherent essential conception, is capable of being made greater or less by the mere way philosophical truths are put forward. Philosophical exposition, faithfully following its insight into the nature of speculative truth, must retain the dialectical form, and exclude everything which is not grasped conceptually and is conception.

78. Just as much as in the procedure of ratiocination, the study of philosophy finds obstruction, too, in the unreasoning conceit that builds itself on well-established truths, which the possessor considers he has no need to return upon and reconsider, but rather takes to be fundamental, and thinks he can by means thereof propound as well as decide and pass sentence. In this regard, it is especially needful to make once again a serious business of philosophy. In all spheres of science, art, skill, and handicraft it is never doubted that, in order to master them, a considerable amount of trouble must be spent in learning and in being trained. As regards philosophy, on the

contrary, there seems still an assumption prevalent that, though every one with eyes and fingers is not on that account in a position to make shoes if he only has leather and a last, yet everybody understands how to philosophize straight away, and pass judgment on philosophy, simply because he possesses the criterion for doing so in his natural reason—as if he did not in the same way possess the standard for shoemaking too in his own foot. It seems as if the possession of philosophy lay just in the want of knowledge and study, as if philosophy left off where the latter began. It is commonly held to be a formal kind of knowledge devoid of all substantial content. There is a general failure to perceive that, in the case of any knowledge and any science, what is taken for truth, even as regards content, can only deserve the name of "truth" when philosophy has had a hand in its production. Let the other sciences try as much as they like to get along by ratiocination or *raisonnement* without philosophy, they are unable to keep alive without it, or to have any spiritual significance and truth in them.

79. As regards philosophy in its proper and genuine sense, we find put forward without any hesitation, as an entirely sufficient equivalent for the long course of mental discipline—for that profound and fruitful process through which the human spirit attains to knowledge—the direct revelation of the divine and the healthy common sense of mankind, unconcerned with and undisciplined by any other knowledge or by proper philosophical reflection. These are held to be a good substitute for real philosophy, much in the way that chicory is lauded as a substitute for coffee. It is not a very pleasing spectacle to observe uncultivated ignorance and crudity of mind, with neither form nor taste, without the capacity to concentrate its thoughts on an abstract proposition, still less on a connected statement of such propositions, confidently proclaiming itself to be intellectual freedom and toleration, and even the inspiration of genius. This last used once upon a time, as everyone knows, to be all the vogue in the case of poetry, as it is now in philosophy. Instead of poetry, however,

the efforts of this form of inspiration, when it had any sense at all, resulted in the production of trivial prose, or, if it went beyond that, it produced raving harangues. In the same way here in the case of philosophy; philosophizing by the light of nature, which thinks itself too good for conceptual thinking, and, because of the want of it, takes itself to have direct intuitive ideas and poetical thoughts,—such philosophizing trades in arbitrary combinations of an imagination merely disorganized through thinking—fictitious creations that are neither fish nor flesh, neither poetry nor philosophy.

80. On the other hand again, when instinctive philosophy follows the more secure course prescribed by healthy common sense, it treats us to a rhetorical *mélange* of commonplace truths. When it is charged with the triviality of what it offers, it assures us, in reply, that the fullness and richness of its meaning lie deep down in its own heart, and that others must feel this too, since with such phrases as the "heart's natural innocence," "purity of conscience," and so on, it supposes it has expressed things that are ultimate and final, to which no one can take exception, and about which nothing further can be required. But the very problem in hand was just that the best must not be left behind hidden away in secret, but be brought out of the depths and set forth in the light of day. It could quite well from the start have spared itself the trouble of bringing forward ultimate and final truths of that sort; they were long since to be found, say, in the Catechism, in popular proverbs, etc. It is an easy matter to grasp such truths in their indefinite and crooked inaccurate form, and in many cases to point out that the mind convinced of them is conscious of the very opposite truths. When it struggles to get itself out of the mental embarrassment thereby produced, it will tumble into further confusion, and possibly burst out with the assertion that in short and in fine the matter is settled, the truth is so and so, and anything else is mere "sophistry"— a password used by plain common sense against cultivated critical reason, like the phrase "visionary dreaming," by which those ignorant of philosophy sum up its character once

for all. Since the man of common sense appeals to his feeling, to an oracle within his breast, he is done with any one who does not agree. He has just to explain that he has no more to say to any one who does not find and feel the same as himself. In other words, he tramples the roots of humanity underfoot. For the nature of humanity is to impel men to agree with one another, and its very existence lies simply in the explicit realization of a community of conscious life. What is anti-human, the condition of mere animals, consists in keeping within the sphere of feeling pure and simple, and in being able to communicate only by way of feeling-states.

81. When a man asks for a royal road to science,[42] no more convenient and comfortable way can be mentioned to him than to put his trust in "healthy common sense." And for the rest, to keep abreast of the times and advance with philosophy, let him read reviews of philosophical works, and even go the length of reading the prefaces and first paragraphs of the works themselves; for the latter give the general principles on which everything turns, while the reviews along with the historical notice provide over and above the critical judgment and appreciation, which, being a judgment passed on the work, goes farther than the work that is judged. This common way a man can take in his dressing-gown. But spiritual elation in the eternal, the sacred, the infinite, moves along the highway of truth in the robes of the high priest—a road that, from the first, is itself immediate being in its innermost, the inspiration of profound and original ideas and flashes of elevated thought. All the same, those depths do not yet reveal the wellspring of inner reality; nor, again, are these sky-rockets the empyrean. True thoughts and scientific insight can only be

[42]A phrase derived from a remark attributed to Euclid in a story handed down by Proclus, a Neoplatonic philosopher (410–485 A.D.). It seems that when the Egyptian King Ptolemy I wished to learn geometry but was disinclined to master the many books of Euclid's *Elements*, Euclid replied to his royal highness that "there is no royal road to geometry."

won by the labor of the notion. Conceptions alone can produce universality in the knowing process. This universality is critically developed and completely finished knowledge. It is not the common indefiniteness and inadequacy of ordinary intelligence. Nor, again, is it that extraordinary kind of universality where the powers and potencies of reason are spoiled and ruined by genius through indolence and self-conceit. It is truth which has successfully reached its own inherent native form. It is this universality which is capable of being the property of every self-conscious reason.

82. Since I have taken the self-development of the notion to be the medium wherein science really exists, and since in those respects to which I have drawn attention, as well as in others, current ideas about the nature of truth and the shape it assumes deviate from my view, and indeed are quite opposed to my position, the consideration of this divergence of view does not seem to promise well for a favorable reception of an attempt to expound the system of science in this sense. In the meantime, I may call to mind that while, e.g., the supreme merit of Plato's philosophy has sometimes been held to consist in his myths which are scientifically valueless, there have also been times, spoken of even as times of mere sentimental enthusiasm, when the Aristotelian philosophy has been respected on account of its speculative depth of insight, and when the *Parmenides* of Plato—perhaps the greatest literary product of ancient dialectic—has been taken to be the positive expression of the divine life, the unveiling and disclosing of its inmost truth. I may reflect, too, that notwithstanding much cloudy obscurity which was the product of ecstasy, this misunderstood ecstasy was in point of fact meant to be nothing else than the activity of the pure notion; furthermore, that what is best in the philosophy of our time takes its value to lie in its scientific character; and that, even though others take a different view, it is only in virtue of its scientific character that recent philosophy really gains validity and acceptance. Thus, then, I may hope too that this attempt to justify the claim of science to be a conceptual process, and systematically to de-

velop and present science in this its own peculiar medium, will manage to make a way for itself by the inherent truth of the result accomplished. We may rest assured that it is the nature of truth to force its way to recognition when the time comes, and that it only appears when its time has come, and hence never appears too soon, and never finds a public that is not ripe to receive it. And, further, we may be sure that the individual thinker requires this result to take place, in order to give him confidence in regard to what is no more as yet than a matter for himself singly and alone, and in order to find his assurance, which in the first instance merely belongs to a particular individual, realized as something universal. In this connection, however, it is very often necessary to distinguish the public from those who take upon themselves to be its representatives and spokesmen. The public takes up an attitude in many respects quite different from the latter, indeed, even opposed to them. Whereas the public goodnaturedly and generously will rather take the blame upon itself when a philosophical work is not quite acceptable or intelligible to it, these "representatives," on the contrary, convinced of their own competence, put all the blame on the authors. The influence of the work on the public is more silent than the action of those "representatives," who are like the dead burying their dead.[43] While the general level of insight at the present time is in the main more highly cultivated, its curiosity more quickened and alert, and its judgment more swiftly made up and pronounced, so that the feet of those who will carry you out are already at the door:[44] at the same time we have often to distinguish from all this the slower and more gradual effect which rectifies the direction of attention caught and compelled by imposing assurances, corrects, too, contemptuous censure, and after a little provides a contemporary audience for one part, while another after a temporary vogue finds no audience with posterity any longer.

[43]See the Gospel according to St. Matthew, 8:22.
[44]See the Acts of the Apostles, 5:9.

83. For the rest, at a time when the universal nature of spiritual life has become so very much emphasized and strengthened, and the mere individual aspect has become, as it should be, correspondingly a matter of indifference, when, too, that universal aspect holds, by the entire range of its substance, the full measure of the wealth it has built up, and lays claim to it all, the share in the total work of mind that falls to the activity of any particular individual can only be very small. Because this is so, the individual must all the more forget himself, as in fact the very nature of science implies and requires that he should; and he must, moreover, become and do what he can. But all the less must be demanded of him, just as he can expect the less from himself, and may ask the less for himself.

INTRODUCTION

1. It is natural to suppose that, before philosophy enters upon its subject proper—namely, the actual knowledge of what truly is—it is necessary to come first to an understanding concerning knowledge, which is looked upon as the instrument by which to take possession of the Absolute, or as the means through which to get a sight of it.[45] The apprehension seems legitimate, on the one hand that there may be various kinds of knowledge, among which one might be better adapted than another for the attainment of our purpose—and thus a wrong choice is possible: on the other hand again that, since knowing is a faculty of a definite kind and with a determinate range, without the more precise determination of its nature and limits we might take hold on clouds of error instead of the heaven of truth.

2. This apprehensiveness is sure to pass even into the conviction that the whole enterprise which sets out to secure for consciousness by means of knowledge what exists *per se*, is in its very nature absurd; and that between knowledge and the Absolute there lies a boundary which completely cuts off the one from the other. For if knowledge is the instrument by which to get possession of absolute Reality, the suggestion immediately occurs that the application of an instrument to anything does *not* leave it as it is for itself, but rather entails in the process, and has in view, a molding and alteration of it. Or, again, if knowledge is not an instrument which we actively employ, but a kind of passive medium through which the light of the truth reaches us, then here, too, we do not receive it as it is in itself, but as it is through and in this medium. In either case we employ a means which immediately brings about the very opposite of its own end; or, rather, the absurdity lies in

[45]This refers to the approach to philosophy proposed by Kant, and before him by the school of British Empiricists beginning with John Locke (1632–1704). See especially Kant's prefaces to the first and second editions of his *Critique of Pure Reason*, and to Locke's "Epistle to the Reader" at the beginning of his *Essay Concerning Human Understanding*.

making use of any means at all. It seems indeed open to us to find in the knowledge of the way in which the *instrument* operates, a remedy for this parlous state; for thereby it becomes possible to remove from the result the part which, in our idea of the Absolute received through that instrument, belongs to the instrument, and thus to get the truth in its purity. But this improvement would, as a matter of fact, only bring us back to the point where we were before. If we take away again from a definitely formed thing that which the instrument has done in the shaping of it, then the thing (in this case the Absolute) stands before us once more just as it was previous to all this trouble, which, as we now see, was superfluous. If the Absolute were only to be brought on the whole nearer to us by this agency, without any change being wrought in it, like a bird caught by a limestick, it would certainly scorn a trick of that sort, if it were not in its very nature, and did it not wish to be, beside us from the start. For a trick is what knowledge in such a case would be, since by all its busy toil and trouble it gives itself the air of doing something quite different from bringing about a relation that is merely immediate, and so a waste of time to establish. Or, again, if the examination of knowledge, which we represent as a medium, makes us acquainted with the law of its refraction, it is likewise useless to eliminate this refraction from the result. For knowledge is not the divergence of the ray, but the ray itself by which the truth comes in contact with us; and if this be removed, the bare direction or the empty place would alone be indicated.

3. Meanwhile, if the fear of falling into error introduces an element of distrust into science, which without any scruples of that sort goes to work and actually does know, it is not easy to understand why, conversely, a distrust should not be placed in this very distrust, and why we should not take care lest the fear of error is not just the initial error. As a matter of fact, this fear presupposes something, indeed a great deal, as truth, and supports its scruples and consequences on what should itself be examined beforehand to see whether it is truth. It starts

with ideas of knowledge as an instrument, and as a medium; and presupposes a distinction of ourselves from this knowledge. More especially it takes for granted that the Absolute stands on one side, and that knowledge on the other side, by itself and cut off from the Absolute, is still something real; in other words, that knowledge, which, by being outside the Absolute, is certainly also outside truth, is nevertheless true—a position which, while calling itself fear of error, makes itself known rather as fear of the truth.

4. This conclusion comes from the fact that the Absolute alone is true or that the True is alone absolute. It may be set aside by making the distinction that a knowledge which does not indeed know the Absolute as science wants to do, is none the less true too; and that knowledge in general, though it may possibly be incapable of grasping the Absolute, can still be capable of truth of another kind. But we shall see as we proceed that random talk like this leads in the long run to a confused distinction between an absolute truth and a truth of some other sort, and that "absolute," "knowledge," and so on, are words which presuppose a meaning that has first to be got at.

5. With such like useless ideas and expressions about knowledge, as an instrument to take hold of the Absolute, or as a medium through which we have a glimpse of truth, and so on (relations to which all these ideas of a knowledge which is divided from the Absolute and an Absolute divided from knowledge in the last resort lead), we need not concern ourselves. Nor need we trouble about the evasive pretexts which create the incapacity of science out of the presupposition of such relations, in order at once to be rid of the toil of science, and to assume the air of serious and zealous effort about it. Instead of being troubled with giving answers to all these, they may be straightway rejected as adventitious and arbitrary ideas; and the use which is here made of words like "absolute," "knowledge," as also "objective" and "subjective," and innumerable others, whose meaning is assumed to be familiar to everyone, might well be regarded as so much deception.

For to give out that their significance is universally familiar and that everyone indeed possesses their notion, rather looks like an attempt to dispense with the only important matter, which is just to give this notion. With better right, on the contrary, we might spare ourselves the trouble of taking any notice at all of such ideas and ways of talking which would have the effect of warding off science altogether; for they make a mere empty show of knowledge which at once vanishes when science comes on the scene.

6. But science, in the very fact that it comes on the scene, is itself a phenomenon; its "coming on the scene" is not yet *itself* carried out in all the length and breadth of its truth. In this regard, it is a matter of indifference whether we consider that it (science) is the phenomenon because it makes its appearance alongside another kind of knowledge, or call that other untrue knowledge its process of appearing. Science, however, must liberate itself from this phenomenality, and it can only do so by turning against it. For science cannot simply reject a form of knowledge which is not true, and treat this as a common view of things, and then assure us that itself is an entirely different kind of knowledge, and holds the other to be of no account at all; nor can it appeal to the fact that in this other there are presages of a better. By giving that assurance it would declare its force and value to lie in its bare existence; but the untrue knowledge appeals likewise to the fact that it *is*, and assures us that to it *science* is nothing. One barren assurance, however, is of just as much value as another. Still less can science appeal to the presages of a better, which are to be found present in untrue knowledge and are there pointing the way towards science; for it would, on the one hand, be appealing again in the same way to a merely existent fact; and, on the other, it would be appealing to itself, to the way in which it exists in untrue knowledge, i.e. to a bad form of its own existence, to its appearance, rather than to its real and true nature (*an und für sich*). For this reason we shall here undertake the exposition of knowledge as a phenomenon.

7. Now because this exposition has for its object only phenomenal knowledge, the exposition itself seems not to be science, free, self-moving in the shape proper to itself, but may, from this point of view, be taken as the pathway of the natural consciousness which is pressing forward to true knowledge. Or it can be regarded as the path of the soul, which is traversing the series of its own forms of embodiment, like stages appointed for it by its own nature, that it may possess the clearness of spiritual life when, through the complete experience of its own self, it arrives at the knowledge of what it is in itself.

8. Natural consciousness will prove itself to be only knowledge in principle or not real knowledge. Since, however, it immediately takes itself to be the real and genuine knowledge, this pathway has a negative significance for it; what is a realization of the notion of knowledge means for it rather the ruin and overthrow of itself; for on this road it loses its own truth. Because of that, the road can be looked on as the path of doubt, or more properly a highway of despair. For what happens there is not what is usually understood by doubting, a jostling against this or that supposed truth, the outcome of which is again a disappearance in due course of the doubt and a return to the former truth, so that at the end the matter is taken as it was before. On the contrary, that pathway is the conscious insight into the untruth of the phenomenal knowledge, for which that is the most real which is after all only the unrealized notion. On that account, too, this thorough-going skepticism is not what doubtless earnest zeal for truth and science fancies it has equipped itself with in order to be ready to deal with them—viz. the *resolve*, in science, not to deliver itself over to the thoughts of others on their mere authority, but to examine everything for itself, and only follow its own conviction, or, still better, to produce everything itself and hold only its own act for true.

9. The series of shapes, which consciousness traverses on this road, is rather the detailed history of the process of train-

ing and educating consciousness itself up to the level of science.[46] That resolve presents this mental development (*Bildung*) in the simple form of an intended purpose, as immediately finished and complete, as having taken place; this pathway, on the other hand, is, as opposed to this abstract intention, or untruth, the actual carrying out of that process of development. To follow one's own conviction is certainly more than to hand oneself over to authority; but by the conversion of opinion held on authority into opinion held out of personal conviction, the content of what is held is not necessarily altered, and truth has not thereby taken the place of error. If we stick to a system of opinion and prejudice resting on the authority of others, or upon personal conviction, the one differs from the other merely in the conceit which animates the latter. Skepticism, directed to the whole compass of phenomenal consciousness, on the contrary, makes mind for the first time qualified to test what truth is; since it brings about a despair regarding what are called natural views, thoughts, and opinions, which it is matter of indifference to call personal or belonging to others, and with which the consciousness, that proceeds straight away to criticize and test, is still filled and hampered, thus being, as a matter of fact, incapable of what it wants to undertake.

10. The completeness of the forms of unreal consciousness will be brought about precisely through the necessity of the advance and the necessity of their connection with one another. To make this comprehensible we may remark, by way of preliminary, that the exposition of untrue consciousness in its untruth is not a merely negative process. Such a one-sided view of it is what the natural consciousness generally adopts;

---

[46]Hegel's discussion of the "path of doubt" and "highway of dispair" that leads up to "the level of science" is reminiscent of Plato's account of the "ascent of the soul to the mind" as found in his famous metaphor of the cave (*Republic*, 518a–518c). The path, in both instances, is not a pleasant one.

and a knowledge, which makes this one-sidedness its essence, is one of those shapes assumed by incomplete consciousness which falls into the course of the inquiry itself and will come before us there. For this view is skepticism, which always sees in the result only pure nothingness, and abstracts from the fact that this nothing is determinate, is the nothing of *that out of which* it comes as a result. Nothing, however, is only, in fact, the true result, when taken as the nothing of what it comes from; it is thus itself a determinate nothing, and has a *content*. The skepticism which ends with the abstraction "nothing" or "emptiness" can advance from this not a step farther, but must wait and see whether there is possibly anything new offered, and what that is—in order to cast it into the same abysmal void. When once, on the other hand, the result is apprehended, as it truly is, as *determinate* negation, a new form has thereby immediately arisen; and in the negation the transition is made by which the progress through the complete succession of forms comes about of itself.

11. The goal, however, is fixed for knowledge just as necessarily as the succession in the process. The terminus is at that point where knowledge is no longer compelled to go beyond itself, where it finds its own self, and the notion corresponds to the object and the object to the notion. The progress towards this goal consequently is without a halt, and at no earlier stage is satisfaction to be found. That which is confined to a life of nature is unable of itself to go beyond its immediate existence; but by something other than itself it is forced beyond that; and to be thus wrenched out of its setting is its death. Consciousness, however, is to itself its own notion; thereby it immediately transcends what is limited, and, since this latter belongs to it, consciousness transcends its own self. Along with the particular there is at the same time set up the "beyond," were this only, as in spatial intuition, *beside* what is limited. Consciousness, therefore, suffers this violence at its own hands; it destroys its own limited satisfaction. When feeling of violence, anxiety for the truth may well withdraw,

and struggle to preserve for itself that which is in danger of being lost. But it can find no rest.[47] Should that anxious fearfulness wish to remain always in unthinking indolence, thought will agitate the thoughtlessness, its restlessness will disturb that indolence. Or let it take its stand as a form of sentimentality which assures us it finds everything good in its kind, and this assurance likewise will suffer violence at the hands of reason, which finds something *not* good just because and in so far as it is a *kind*. Or, again, fear of the truth may conceal itself from itself and others behind the pretext that precisely burning zeal for the very truth makes it so difficult, nay impossible, to find any other truth except that of which alone vanity is capable—that of being ever so much cleverer than any ideas, which one gets from oneself or others, could make possible. This sort of conceit which understands how to belittle every truth and turn away from it back into itself, and gloats over this its own private understanding, which always knows how to dissipate every possible thought, and to find, instead of all the content, merely the barren Ego—this is a satisfaction which must be left to itself; for it flees the universal and seeks only an isolated existence on its own account (*Fürsichseyn*).

12. As the foregoing has been stated, provisionally and in general, concerning the manner and the necessity of the process of the inquiry, it may also be of further service to make some observations regarding the method of carrying this out. This exposition, viewed as a process of relating science to phenomenal knowledge, and as an inquiry and critical examination into the reality of knowing, does not seem able to be effected without some presupposition which is laid down as an ultimate criterion. For an examination consists in applying an accepted standard, and, on the final agreement or disagreement therewith of what is tested, deciding whether the latter is right or wrong; and the standard in general, and so science,

---

[47]Hegel might have had in mind the famous statement of St. Augustine, "Our hearts are restless until they rest in Thee." *Confessions*, bk. I, sec. 1.

were this the criterion, is thereby accepted as the essence or inherently real (*Ansich*). But, here, where science first appears on the scene, neither science nor any sort of standard has justified itself as the essence or ultimate reality; and without this no examination seems able to be instituted.

13. This contradiction and the removal of it will become more definite if, to begin with, we call to mind the abstract determinations of knowledge and of truth as they are found in consciousness. Consciousness, we find, *distinguishes* from itself something, to which at the same time it *relates* itself; or, to use the current expression, there is something *for* consciousness; and the determinate form of this process of relating, or of there being something for a consciousness, is knowledge. But from this being for another we distinguish being in itself or *per se*; what is related to knowledge is likewise distinguished from it, and posited as also existing outside this relation; the aspect of being *per se* or in itself is called Truth. What really lies in these determinations does not further concern us here; for since the object of our inquiry is phenomenal knowledge, its determinations are also taken up, in the first instance, as they are immediately offered to us. And they are offered to us very much in the way we have just stated.

14. If now our inquiry deals with the truth of knowledge, it appears that we are inquiring what knowledge is in itself. But in this inquiry knowledge is *our* object, it is *for us*; and the essential nature (*Ansich*) of knowledge, were this to come to light, would be rather its being *for us*: what we should assert to be its essence would rather be, not the truth of knowledge, but only our knowledge of it. The essence or the criterion would lie in us; and that which was to be compared with this standard, and on which a decision was to be passed as a result of this comparison, would not necessarily have to recognize that criterion.

15. But the nature of the object which we are examining surmounts this separation, or semblance of separation, and presupposition. Consciousness furnishes its own criterion in itself, and the inquiry will thereby be a comparison of itself

with its own self; for the distinction, just made, falls inside itself. In consciousness there is one element *for* an other, or, in general, consciousness implicates the specific character of the moment of knowledge. At the same time this "other" is to consciousness not merely *for it*, but also outside this relation, or has a being in itself, i.e. there is the moment of truth. Thus in what consciousness inside itself declares to be the essence or truth we have the standard which itself sets up, and by which we are to measure its knowledge. Suppose we call knowledge the notion, and the essence or truth "being" or the object, then the examination consists in seeing whether the notion corresponds with the object. But if we call the inner nature of the object, or what it is in itself, the notion, and, on the other side, understand by object the notion *qua* object, i.e., the way the notion is *for* an other, then the examination consists in our seeing whether the object corresponds to its own notion. It is clear, of course, that both of these processes are the same. The essential fact, however, to be borne in mind throughout the whole inquiry is that both these moments, notion and object, "being for another" and "being in itself," themselves fall within that knowledge which we are examining. Consequently we do not require to bring standards with us, nor to apply *our* fancies and thoughts in the inquiry; and just by our leaving these aside we are enabled to treat and discuss the subject as it actually is in itself and for itself, as it is in its complete reality.

16. But not only in this respect, that notion and object, the criterion and what is to be tested, are ready to hand in consciousness itself, is any addition of ours superfluous, but we are also spared the trouble of comparing these two and of making an examination in the strict sense of the term; so that in this respect, too, since consciousness tests and examines itself, all we are left to do is simply and solely to look on. For consciousness is, on the one hand, consciousness of the object, on the other, consciousness of itself; consciousness of what to it is true, and consciousness of its knowledge of that truth. Since both are for the same consciousness, it is itself

their comparison; it is the same consciousness that decides and knows whether its knowledge of the object corresponds with this object or not. The object, it is true, appears only to be in such wise for consciousness as consciousness knows it. Consciousness does not seem able to get, so to say, behind it as it is, not for consciousness, but in itself, and consequently seems also unable to test knowledge by it. But just because consciousness has, in general, knowledge of an object, there is already present the distinction that the inherent nature, what the object is in itself, is one thing to consciousness, while knowledge, or the being of the object *for* consciousness, is another moment. Upon this distinction, which is present as a fact, the examination turns. Should both, when thus compared, not correspond, consciousness seems bound to alter its knowledge, in order to make it fit the object. But in the alteration of the knowledge, the object itself also, in point of fact, is altered; for the knowledge which existed was essentially a knowledge of the object; with change in the knowledge, the object also becomes different, since it belonged essentially to this knowledge. Hence consciousness comes to find that what formerly to it was the essence is not what is *per se*, or what was *per se* was only *per se for consciousness*. Since, then, in the case of its object consciousness finds its knowledge not corresponding with this object, the object likewise fails to hold out; or the standard for examining is altered when that, whose criterion this standard was to be, does not hold its ground in the course of the examination; and the examination is not only an examination of knowledge, but also of the criterion used in the process.

17. This dialectic process which consciousness executes on itself—on its knowledge as well as on its object—in the sense that out of it the new and true object arises, is precisely what is termed Experience. In this connection, there is a moment in the process just mentioned which should be brought into more decided prominence, and by which a new light is cast on the scientific aspect of the following exposition. Consciousness knows something; this something is the

essence or what is *per se*. This object, however, is also the *per se*, the inherent reality, *for consciousness*. Hence comes ambiguity of this truth. Consciousness, as we see, has now two objects; one is the first *per se*, the second is the existence *for consciousness* of this *per se*. The last object appears at first sight to be merely the reflection of consciousness into itself, i.e., an idea not of an object, but solely of its knowledge of that first object. But, as was already indicated, by that very process the first object is altered; it ceases to be what is *per se*, and becomes consciously something which is *per se* only *for consciousness*. Consequently, then, what this real *per se* is for consciousness is truth: which, however, means that this is the essential reality, or the object which consciousness has. This new object contains the nothingness of the first; the new object is the *experience* concerning that first object.

18. In this treatment of the course of experience, there is an element in virtue of which it does not seem to be in agreement with what is ordinarily understood by experience. The transition from the first object and the knowledge of it to the other object, in regard to which we say we have had experience, was so stated that the knowledge of the first object, the existence *for consciousness* of the first *ens per se*, is itself to be the second object. But it usually seems that we learn by experience the untruth of our first notion by appealing to some other object which we may happen to find casually and externally; so that, in general, what we have is merely the bare and simple apprehension of what is in and for itself. On the view above given, however, the new object is seen to have come about by a transformation or conversion of consciousness itself. This way of looking at the matter is *our* doing, what *we* contribute; by its means the series of experiences through which consciousness passes is lifted into a scientifically constituted sequence, but this does not exist for the consciousness we contemplate and consider. We have here, however, the same sort of circumstance, again, of which we spoke a short time ago when dealing with the relation of this exposition to scepticism, viz. that the result which at any

time comes about in the case of an untrue mode of knowledge cannot possibly collapse into an empty nothing, but must necessarily be taken as the negation of that of which it is a result—a result which contains what truth the preceding mode of knowledge has in it. In the present instance the position takes this form: since what at first appeared as object is reduced, when it passes into consciousness, to what knowledge takes it to be, and the implicit nature, the real in itself, becomes what this entity *per se* is *for consciousness*; this latter is the new object, whereupon there appears also a new mode or embodiment of consciousness, of which the essence is something other than that of the preceding mode. It is this circumstance which carries forward the whole succession of the modes or attitudes of consciousness in their own necessity. It is only this necessity, this origination of the new object— which offers itself to consciousness without consciousness knowing how it comes by it—that to us, who watch the process, is to be seen going on, so to say, behind its back. Thereby there enters into its process a moment of being *per se* or of being for us, which is not expressly presented to that consciousness which is in the grip of experience itself. The *content*, however, of what we see arising, exists for it, and we lay hold of and comprehend merely its formal character, i.e., its *bare* origination; *for it*, what has thus arisen has merely the character of object; while, *for us*, it appears at the same time as a process and coming into being.

19. In virtue of that necessity this pathway to science is itself *eo ipso* science, and is, moreover, as regards its content, Science of the Experience of Consciousness.

20. The experience which consciousness has concerning itself can, by its essential principle, embrace nothing less than the entire system of consciousness, the whole realm of the truth of mind, and in such wise that the moments of truth are set forth in the specific and peculiar character they here possess—i.e., not as abstract pure moments, but as they are for consciousness, or as consciousness itself appears in its relation to them, and in virtue of which they are moments of the

whole, are embodiments or modes of consciousness. In pressing forward to its true form of existence, consciousness will come to a point at which it lays aside its semblance of being hampered with what is foreign to it, with what is only for it and exists as an other; it will reach a position where appearance becomes identified with essence, where, in consequence, its exposition coincides with just this very point, this very stage of the science proper of mind. And, finally, when it grasps this its own essence, it will connote the nature of absolute knowledge itself.